I0004427

DYNAMICS AX TIPS & TRICKS POCKET REFERENCE

Murray Fife

ISBN-13: 978-1539316008

ISBN-10: 1539316009

Preface

What You Need for This Guide

All the examples shown in this blueprint were done with the Microsoft Dynamics AX hosted image that was deployed from the Microsoft Lifecycle Services. The following list of software from the virtual image was leveraged within this guide:

Microsoft Dynamics AX

Even though all the preceding software was used during the development and testing of the recipes in this book, they may also work on earlier versions of the software with minor tweaks and adjustments, and should also work on later versions without any changes.

Errata

Although we have taken every care to ensure the accuracy of our content, mistakes do happen. If you find a mistake in one of our books—maybe a mistake in the text or the code—we would be grateful if you would report this to us. By doing so, you can save other readers from frustration and help us improve subsequent versions of this book. If you find any errata, please report them by emailing editor@dynamicsaxcompanions.com.

Piracy

Piracy of copyright material on the Internet is an ongoing problem across all media. If you come across any illegal copies of our works, in any form, on the Internet, please provide us with the location address or website name immediately so that we can pursue a remedy.

Please contact us at legal@dynamicsaxcompanions.com with a link to the suspected pirated material.

We appreciate your help in protecting our authors, and our ability to bring you valuable content.

Questions

You can contact us at help@dynamicsaxcompanions.com if you are having a problem with any aspect of the book, and we will do our best to address it.

TABLE OF CONTENTS

INTRODUCTION

Dynamics AX is chock full of features that you can implement at the module level, but the true power of the product comes from the boat load of smaller features that are built into the user interface, the modules themselves. Also you can make Dynamics AX even more powerful by taking advantage of the other foundation products such as SharePoint and Office. The real trick is to know that these capabilities are there, and that is what this book is aimed to do.

Even the most seasoned Dynamics AX user or administrator should find a new tip or trick here that will make them look like a rock star.

Topics Covered

- DESKTOP CLIENT TIPS

- FUNCTIONAL TRICKS

- OFFICE TRICKS

- REPORTING TIPS

- WORKFLOW TRICKS

- SYSTEM ADMINISTRATION TIPS

DESKTOP CLIENT TIPS

You don't have to go very far within Dynamics AX to start finding features that can make your work a little easier because the desktop client itself is jam packed with features. You can tweak how the client looks so that you can see just the information that you want to see, and you can also use inbuilt shortcuts within the client to make finding information and getting around the system even easier.

Topics Covered

- Find (almost) anything through the enterprise search

- Personalize Your Ribbon Bar To Make Menu Buttons Easier To Find

- Set The Number Of Autocolumns To Match Your Screen Real Estate

- Add Fields To Summary Tabs For Easy Reference

- Teleport Directly To Maintenance Tabs Using Shortcut Keys

- How Not To Find Something In Dynamics AX

- Press Star To Instantly Lookup Data Values

- Type In Product Names To Find Product Numbers

- Use Shorthand To Enter Dates

- Have Dynamics AX Calculate The Last Day Of The Month For You

- Configuring the Status Bar To Show Just What You Need

- Have Dynamics AX Tell You When There Are Document Attachments

- Make Dynamics AX Less Chatty By Turning Off Infolog Notifications

- Stop Dynamics AX From Warning You Every Time You Switch Companies

- Set Your Home Page To Automatically Refresh

- Change Your Company Through The Status Bar Charm

- Open New Workspaces To Quickly Access Multiple Areas At Once

- Clean Up The Navigation Pad To Show Just The Modules You Need

- Add Entire Menu Item Groups At Once To Your Favorites Menu

- Hide The Navigation And Fact Box Panels For More Workspace

- Filter Your Favorites Menu Item

- Navigate The Ribbon Bar Like A Street Fighter With Shortcut Keys

- Hack Form Selection Criteria For Mass Updates

- Copy Document Attachments From One Record To One Or More Other Records

- Process Multiple Records At Once By Using The Multi-Select Option

- Quickly Filter Your Data Through The Type To Filter Box

- Add New Fields To The Type To Filter Search Form To Find Hard To Find Data

- Use Filter By Selection To Quickly Find Common Records

- Use The Filter by Field To Search For Subsets Of Data Within Columns

- Use The Filter By Grid & Wild Cards To Create More Intricate Queries

- Using The Query Dialog To Create More Advanced Filters

- Setting Forms To Automatically Open In Edit Mode

- Create Open Ended Filters By Using Ranges With No Beginning Or End

- Change The Default Language Within The Rich Client

- If You Don't Like The Way Your Data Looks The Rename It

- Convert Any Record Into A Template

Find (almost) anything through the enterprise search

Have you ever spent time searching through the menu system, trying to find a particular form that you need to run? Or have you ever looked for a certain piece of information in Dynamics AX like a customer, only to realize after searching and searching that it is actually a prospect? Dynamics has a feature called Enterprise Search that should save you a lot of time. All you need to do when you are searching for something is type it into the Search button in the top right corner of the Dynamics AX client, and it will suggest where you can find it.

How it works...

Type in the term that you want to search on in the Enterprise Search field in the top right hand corner of the client.

In this case we want to find anything related to Prospects.

Within the workspace, the Enterprise Search will return back all of the forms that are related to the search that you entered, and also on the right are all of the help topics that may be related to the search as well.

Clicking on any of the topics on the right hand side will open up the help explorer and take you directly to the topic.

Clicking on any of the menu links in the main part of the Enterprise Search window will take you directly to the form.

You can also search for data within Dynamics AX by typing in the keyword that you want to search on.

If there are any records that match, then they will be listed in the main panel of the search results.

If you click on the link, it will take you directly to the record maintenance form.

Personalize Your Ribbon Bar To Make Menu Buttons Easier To Find

Everyone knows that you can personalize forms within Dynamics AX to show just the fields that you want. But don't forget that you can also personalize the ribbon bars to your own tastes as well, by hiding groups of menu items that you don't use, and also move menu items from one ribbon bar to the other to make them easier to access.

By streamlining your forms, you can get rid of all the kipple that is cluttering up your daily access to Dynamics AX.

How to do it...

Right-mouse-click on the form that you want to personalize the ribbon bar for, and select the Personalize option.

When the Personalization dialog box is displayed, you will notice that there are two main groups in the Layout panel. By default the personalization starts off with the Tab group selected, which allows you to personalize all of the fields and groups in the body of the form.

If you select the ActionPanelHeader group though, you will see all of the buttons and groups for the ribbon bar.

You can hide any of the menu buttons just by overriding the Visible option, and you can also move entire groups of buttons just by dragging and dropping them from one group to another. In this example we moved all of the selling transactions from the Sell ribbon bar to the Customer ribbon bar.

Now all of our transactions are at our fingertips within the Customer ribbon bar group.

Remember though, you can always return back to the default view and remove all of your customizations for the forms just by clicking on the Reset button within the Personalization dialog box.

Set The Number Of Autocolumns To Match Your Screen Real Estate

Just like people, the screens that everyone uses to access Dynamics AX comes in all shapes and sizes. Some are lean and petite with just a modest screen resolution, whilst others are a little bit more bulked up, with more DPI than should be legal. Luckily, when Dynamics AX builds it's screens for you, it not only re-arranges the fields to best match the size of the application window, but it also allows you to specify how many columns it should use when it's trying to lay out the information.

So if you have a smaller screen, you can trim down the screen to show all of the information in one column so that you don't have to scroll left and right in order to see all of the information, and if you have a larger screen, you can use more columns so that you can see more information on the screen and not have a lot of wasted white space.

How to do it...

Click on the navigation options icon in the top right of the Dynamics AX client and select the Auto Columns menu item. From there you will be able to select the number of columns that you want to use for each of the forms.

If you have a smaller screen, then you can show all of the information using 1 column.

If you have a more traditional monitor then you can use 2 columns to lay out the information a little better.

If you have a larger monitor, then why not use 3+ columns and spread out your information over the entire screen.

Add Fields To Summary Tabs For Easy Reference

You might have already noticed the summary fields that show up in the tab bar whenever you open up forms. These allow you to see the values of some of the fields in the group, even when the tab has been collapsed, which reduces the number of clicks that you have to use to find the key information that you are looking for, and also means that you can collapse a lot of the tabs down so that your are not scrolling through multiple pages of information.

You are not limited through to the summary fields that are enabled by default though, you can add almost ay field that you like to the summary tab line just with a couple of clicks. This allows you to see at a glance all of the information that is important to you.

How to do it...

If there is a field within the body of a tab group that you would like to promote to the summary tab line, just right-mouse-click on it and select the Personalize option.

In the properties group, change the Fast tab summary field to Yes and then close down the Personalization form.

You can repeat this process for as many additional fields as you like, and they will be added to the summary bar for you.

Now you can collapse all of the tabs, and you can still see all of the key information at a glance. You only have to expand the tabs if you want to see more details.

Teleport Directly To Maintenance Tabs Using Shortcut Keys

If you live and die by the keyboard, and only touch the mouse as a last resort then opening up a maintenance form within Dynamics AX is probably killing you because there are all of the tabs that you need to open in order to access the grouped data fields if you haven't learnt the shortcut key to jump directly to the tab. All you need to do is press the CTRL key and the tab number that you want to access, and Dynamics will take you directly there without the use of the mouse.

Now you can jump with ease between the different data tabs like you had your very own mouse TARDIS.

How to do it...

If you right-mouse-click on any of the tabs in the document view, and select the Goto Tab menu item, you will be able to go directly to any of the tabs just by selecting them.

But notice all of the shortcut keys that are associated with the tabs. To go to them without having to use the menu, all you need to do is press the CTRL key along with the tab number that you want to open up.

For example, pressing CTRL+5 will take you directly to the Sales Demographics tab within the customers form.

How Not To Find Something In Dynamics AX

The filtering within Dynamics AX is great and it's easy to use to find just the records that you are interested in. But what if you want to filter particular pieces of information out of the query rather than search for particular information.

You can easily do this with the special filter operator "!" (also known as Not) – all you have to do is put this in front of the values that you don't want to return and those records will be filtered out for you.

How to do it...

Open up the form that you want to filter out and open up the filter grid (CTRL+G)

In the filter box, just type in the value that you want to filter out, but add a "!" in the front of it. In this example we used !"" (note the double quotes) to say that we don't want any records that are blank.

Also, you can apply multiple filters by separating them with commas.

Press Star To Instantly Lookup Data Values

If you are a keyboard jockey and hate to use the mouse, then you may think that dropdown lists are the bane of your existence... but they don't have to. You can instantly pull up a list of all the values for the field just by pressing the * key within the field.

You don't need no stinkin' mouse...

How to do it...

To list all of the valid values in a lookup, just press *.

You can also type in the first part of what you are looking for and then press * to return back a filtered list of matches.

Type In Product Names To Find Product Numbers

A lot of the time when you are looking for a product you are looking for it by the product mane, and not the product number. Rather than navigate the drop down list, and then turn on the filter selector, you can just type in the product name, and if there is a unique match then Dynamics AX will swap the name for the correct part code.

Now you can stop memorizing all of those part codes.

How to do it...

You can search for products the old fashioned way by using the drop down list and then trying to search for the product...

Or you can just type in the name of the product that you want to search for in the Item Number field.

If Dynamics AX is able to find a unique match for you then it will replace the product name with the correct item number.

Use Shorthand To Enter Dates

Dynamics AX has a lot of shortcut keys that you can use to navigate around the system and save you from clicking the mouse too much, but in addition there are some shorthand annotations that you can use in the fields to help you with your day to day data entry.

One example of this is that you don't have to specify the full date (i.e. 12/25/2013) when you enter them in. You can use tokens for the current date and also partial dates (i.e. 1225) that will be translated into the full date. When you are trying to get information in as quickly as possible, then this is incredibly useful.

How to do it...

Type "T" into the date field...

And it will be replaced with the date (and time) from the client machine, which is useful if you server is in a different time zone.

Type "D" into the date field...

And it will be replaced with the date (and time) from the server.

Type in a day number i.e. "DD" into the date field...

And it will be replaced with that date for the current month.

Type in a month and day number combination i.e. "MMDD" into the date field...

And it will be replaced with that month and day for the current year.

Type in a month, day and year number combination i.e. "MMDDYY" into the date field...

And it will be replaced with the full date that matches the shorthand.

Have Dynamics AX Calculate The Last Day Of The Month For You

There are a lot of small features within Dynamics AX that can save you time and energy of trying to mentally calculate what you should do. One example of this is to do with entering in dates. If you have ever had to type in a date for the end of a month, and then had to pause to work out of the month has 28, 29, 30, or 31 days. Next time, just use the date of 31, and Dynamics AX will convert the date to the right value.

How to do it...

Type in your month end date with the date of 31.

Dynamics AX will update the date with the corrected date.

Configuring the Status Bar To Show Just What You Need

The Status Bar within the Dynamics AX client is there to give you a quick way to see some of the configuration parameters without adding too much extra clutter to the client. But by default it may show you a little more information than you really need. If you like things to be tidy, and not see information that you're not interested in then you may want to tweak the information that shows on the Status Bar through the System Options.

Like my grandmother used to say… "A tidy status bar is a tidy mind"

How to do it...

By default, a lot of information is shown on the Status Bar.

To configure the Status Bar options, click on the Files menu, select the Tools sub menu, and then the Options menu item.

When the Options dialog box is displayed, you will see all of the options that you can choose to display on the Status Bar.

You can get rid of all of the extra information that you don't want to see and possibly add items that are useful to you just by checking and unchecking the boxes.

Now the Status Bar looks a little tidier.

If you don't want to see the Status Bar at all, then just set the Show status bar option to None.

That will remove the Status Bar giving you a little more space on the screen.

Have Dynamics AX Tell You When There Are Document Attachments

Being able to attach documents to almost any record in Dynamics AX is a great tool to take advantage of because it allows you to move all of those files that you used to store on network shares or in local file folders, and puts them at everyone's fingertips.

You can make it even more useful though by turning on the notification flag for document attachments in the client options, which will tell AX to highlight the documents button whenever there are documents associated with the record that you have selected. Then you will know immediately if there are files that you can browse through.

How to do it...

From the Files menu in the Dynamics AX client, open the Tools submenu, and select the Options menu item.

Then within the General tab of the options, scroll down to the Miscellaneous group and check the Show attachment status checkbox to enable the document notifications.

Now when you look at records where there are no documents attached the Attachments icon will remain the same as it always did.

But if there are attachments associated with the record, it will be highlighted.

Make Dynamics AX Less Chatty By Turning Off Infolog Notifications

Although getting notifications from Dynamics AX about what it is doing, and any problems that it has come across is good, as you start getting more comfortable with the system, it may be just the errors that you are interested in seeing, and you don't want to have to close down the InfoLog box every time a new journal entry is created.

Luckily, there is a setting that will control the level of detail that Dynamics AX shares with you and you can easily tell it that you just want all, some, or no messages as you performing transactions, letting you really get down to business without pop-up boxes appearing.

How to do it...

From the Files menu, select the Tools sub menu, and select the Options menu item.

Within the General tab of the Options dialog box, you can change the detail level of the messages by selecting it from the Detail level drop down within the Infolog group of the Interface Options.

Note: It's probably not a good idea to select the None option, because if there is an error that is stopping you from something on, you won't have any idea that it happened. Error only is a good choice for the expert users.

When you have selected the detail level that you want returned back by the InfoLog then click the Close button to save your preferences.

Stop Dynamics AX From Warning You Every Time You Switch Companies

If you have multiple companies within Dynamics AX, then you will probably have experienced a Infolog box that shows up every time that Dynamics AX changes from one company to another in the background. At first it's useful, but after the fifth, sixth, or one thousandth time it just becomes annoying because you probably know by now that you are in a new company.

If you want to hide the notification, then there is a flag for that.

How to do it...

From the Files menu select the Tools submenu, and then select the Options menu item.

When the Options dialog box is displayed, select the Status bar tab group on the left.

Then uncheck the Warn company accounts changed option check box.

Then click on the Close button to exit the options.

Now this pesky notice will not show up.

Set Your Home Page To Automatically Refresh

The Home page within Dynamics AX is one of the most useful pages there is, because it gives you one place that you can go to in order to see everything that you are interested in. You can make it even more useful by having the page set to automatically refresh periodically so that you don't have to click the F5 button to refresh the page manually.

Now you will always up to date.

How to do it...

From the File menu, select the Tools submenu, and then click on the Options menu item.

When the Options form is displayed, change the Refresh duration value within the Home page settings group of the General tab from 0 to the interval in minutes that you want have your home page refreshed, and then click on the Close button.

Now just wait and it will refresh automatically.

Change Your Company Through The Status Bar Charm

You all probably know how to change the company through the breadcrumb bar, but you can also change the company through the charm on the status bar. This option also gives you the ability to create a new workspace for the new company as well, just in case you need to have them both open at once.

You can now change companies faster than Worzel Gummidge changed his head.

How to do it...

If you look at the status bar of the Dynamics AX client, then you will notice that the current Company is displayed there. Just double click on it.

When the Select Company dialog box is displayed, you will see all of the companies that you have access to and you can just select the new company and click the OK button to switch within your current workspace.

Alternatively, if you want to open up a new workspace for the company that you have selected, and keep your current company workspace open as well, then just click on the New Workspace button.

How easy is that.

Open New Workspaces To Quickly Access Multiple Areas At Once

Sometimes one version of Dynamics AX running on your desktop is just not enough. Rather than reaching for the desktop shortcut to start up another instance of the application, just create a new Workspace. They start up so much faster.

How to do it...

Click on the Windows icon in the top right of the Dynamics AX client, and select the New Workspace menu item (or press CTRL+W).

This will open up a new independent workspace that you can work with in addition to the original workspace.

Clean Up The Navigation Pad To Show Just The Modules You Need

The good thing about Dynamics AX is that you get all the available modules automatically. The downside is that you get all the available modules automatically. You may not want to see the General Ledger, or Accounts Payable modules, all you may be interested in may just be the Distribution modules.

You can quickly make your life a little less cluttered just by editing your Navigation Pad and hiding all of the modules that you don't need. You can still get to the functionality, just you don't need to wade through the other modules when trying to get to the menu items that you use every day.

How to do it...

Click on the >> button at the bottom right of the Navigation Pad to see all of the additional modules, and then click on the Navigation Pane Options menu item.

When the Navigation Pane Options window is displayed, you will see all of the modules that you have access to, and to remove them from the navigation pane, you just need to uncheck them.

When you have finished doing that, click on the OK button.

Now your Navigation Pane will look a lot tidier and you will have quick access to just the menu items that you are interested in.

Also, this applies to the dropdown from the breadcrumb bar.

Add Entire Menu Item Groups At Once To Your Favorites Menu

Everyone is probably very familiar with the Favorites menu, and knows that you can add any menu item that you like there with just a click of the mouse. Did you know that you can also add groups of menu items as well, that copies all of the structure from the area page menu group over to your favorites as well.

By doing this you can avoid having to spend all that time creating your own personal menu groups in the favorites because they have already been grouped within the area page for you.

How to do it...

Right-mouse-click on the menu heading that you want to add to your favorites and select the Add to Favorites option. In this case I selected the Common group of the Sales and Marketing.

Now when you open up your favorites, the entire sub-menu will be there, including all of the child menu items.

If you want to get rid of some of the submenus, then you can right-mouse-click on the My Favorites menu group, and select the Organize favorites option, which will show you the Organize favorites maintenance form.

Once you have tweaked the menu structure to show just the information that you want then click on the Close button to save your changes.

Now you will have all the menu items that you need from the area page group without having to add them all individually.

Hide The Navigation And Fact Box Panels For More Workspace

Although it's good to see the Navigation Bar and the Fact Box panes within Dynamics AX, sometimes you just need a little space so that you can see all the information that you are working on. That's OK though because you can turn those pane on and off through the View options within the Dynamics AX client.

Now all of you that are shouting "Show me the data!" can get back to work.

How to do it...

Open up the View options, either by clicking on it in the top right-hand corner of the Dynamics AX client, or by pressing ALT-V. From there you can toggle off the Fact pane and the Navigation pane just by selecting them.

Now you have more space on your desktop.

Filter Your Favorites Menu Item

You all probably know that you can add any menu item link to your own personal favorites menu, but you don't have to stop there. You can personalize those favorites also to automatically apply a filter so that you get just the records back that you need.

By doing this, you can create multiple favorite links to the same menu item that returns different sets of data depending on what you are working on, saving you a few extra steps.

How to do it...

Start off by opening up the form that you want to create the favorites shortcut for, and filter the form to just the records that you want to have selected.

From the Filter menu, select the Save as Filter menu item.

Then give your filter a Name and click the OK button to save the filter.

Now right-mouse-click on the parent form, and select the Add to favorites menu item.

When the Add favorite dialog box is displayed, give your new favorite link a name, and then select the Query that you just created from the dropdown box.

When you have done that, click on the OK button to save the filtered favorite.

You can create multiple links to the same form, each with their own filters, so that you can quickly go to just the records that you want.

Navigate The Ribbon Bar Like A Street Fighter With Shortcut Keys

There are two types of users in the world. Those that are attached to their mouse and want to click through the application, and those that are attached to the keyboard and want to use shortcut keys to do everything. For the latter group, don't worry, you can navigate through Dynamics AX just as quickly with the keyboard.

With combo keys at your disposal you will be kicking butt like Ken & Ryu.

How to do it...

Start off by opening up the form that you want to navigate though. In this case we will use the shortcut keys to create a new Sales Order.

Press the ALT key and all of the shortcut options will be displayed on the screen. The first set will be for all of the ribbon bars and also all of the main groups within the selected ribbon bar.

Press N to select the New group of the Sales Order ribbon bar.

The shortcut options will change to just show the items that are within the group that you selected.

Press S.

This will restrict the selections now to just the ones beginning with S. Note here that there are multiple options available. If you didn't want the Sales Order, then you can press S again to toggle to the next S option.

When you are on the right menu icon, just press Enter.

Now you will be in the Create Sales Order dialog box. Now all you have to remember for the next time that you want to create a new Sales Order is:

ALT, N, S, ENTER

How Easy is that!

Hack Form Selection Criteria For Mass Updates

Every now and then you may come across an update that has been designed to be performed one record at a time, and you have 10's, 100's, or even 1000's of records that you want to update at once. Even though it seems like all hope is lost and that you are going to end up with carpel tunnel syndrome from too many mouse clicks, it's not a bleak as you think.

There is a way that you can usually hack the selection query that is used by default for the form to widen up the range of records that will be updated at once. And it's pretty easy to do as well.

How to do it...

On some forms, if you select one record then you are able to use the menu items.

But if you select multiple records, then the menu's are disabled.

Select one record and click on the menu item that you want to apply to all of the records = in this case the Print option for the Interest Notes. Notice the selection criteria in the dialog form shows the record that will be used for this update.

Click on the Select button to change the selection criteria.

When the selection query editor is displayed you will be able to see the selection criteria records again.

Blank out the fields that you don't want to filter on to open up the selection to a wider range of records and then click on the OK button.

When you return to the selection dialog box you will notice that those field selections are now blank. Just click on the OK button to continue.

This will now perform the action that was only being allowed to be applied to the single record to all of the records that match the search range.

Copy Document Attachments From One Record To One Or More Other Records

Document attachments are a great feature within Dynamics AX, because it allows you to attach notes and files to almost any piece of data within the system. But don't reattach the same document over and over again if it applies to multiple records, use the copy and paste option that is built into the Document Management feature.

It's not plagiarizing to copy documents, it's just more efficient.

How to do it...

To copy an attachment from one record to another, open up the Document Handling form, select the attachments, and then select the Copy option from the Functions menu.

Then open up the Document Attachments form for the record that you want to attach the document to, and select the Paste option from the Functions menu.

Now the document should be associated with the target record.

If you want to paste the attachment against multiple records at once, just select all of the records, open up the Document Attachments form, and then select the Paste To All option from within the Functions menu.

Now all of the selected records will have the document attached to them.

How easy is that.

Process Multiple Records At Once By Using The Multi-Select Option

A lot of the time you are not just working on one record at a time, you are processing batches of records. For example, you may be releasing multiple orders to picking, confirming multiple purchase orders, or printing multiple order confirmations. Dynamics AX makes this easy as pie to do because a lot of the time, you can use the multiple selection option to choose the records that you want to perform the same action on, and then it will work through them one at a time so that you don't have to.

Say goodbye to being stuck in the Groundhog Day equivalent of single record processing.

How to do it...

In this example we will show how you can generate multiple order confirmations with just the click of the button.

Just select all of the orders that you want to print, and then click on the Confirmation button within the Generate group of the Sell ribbon bar.

When the Confirm Sales Order dialog box is displayed, all of the orders will be shown in the detail section. All you need to do is click the OK button.

Now all of the order confirmations will be created.

If you used the email, or automatic printing option then this process would look a lot less cluttered ☺

Quickly Filter Your Data Through The Type To Filter Box

If you want to quickly filter list pages to show you just the records that you are interested in then Dynamics AX provides a Type to Filter option on almost all of the main forms. All you need to do is type in what you are looking for, and it will do the rest for you.

Getting rid of all the data that you don't want has never been so easy.

How to do it...

To filter your data, start off by clicking on the combo box to the right of the Type to Filter field, and selecting the field that you would like to filter on. All of the fields that are shown on the list page will be listed here.

Then just select the Type to Filter field either by clicking on it with the mouse, or by using the SHIFT+F3 shortcut key, and then type in the key words that you want to filter your current list page on.

As soon as you press the Enter key, your view will be filtered, and return all records where the field contains your filter term.

Note: You won't have to type in any wild cards or use any placeholders in the search.

How simple is that?

Add New Fields To The Type To Filter Search Form To Find Hard To Find Data

The Type To Filter search option is super useful, but you are not limited to just the default fields that show up on the list page. If you want to search based on additional fields, then all you need to do is add them to the search criteria and then start searching.

No data is able to hide from you now.

How to do it...

If you want to filter on a field that does not show up by default in the combo box to the right of the Type to Filter field, just click on the More option at the bottom of the list.

This will open up the Select Fields dialog box that will show you all of the tables that are related to the list page that you are currently in.

If you expand out the tables in the Select Fields dialog box, then you can select any additional field and then click the Add button.

After you have added all of the additional search fields, then just close the form.

When you return to the list page, you will see all of the additional search fields have been added to the list page, and can also now be selected from the field drop down selector.

All you have to do in order to filter out based on the new fields is type in your search value, and the list page will be filtered.

Isn't that too cool?

Use Filter By Selection To Quickly Find Common Records

Filtering your list pages is even easier if you have an example of a record already on the page that matches what you are searching for because you can use it as a template for your search and use the Filter By Selection feature to find all of the other records that match, saving you a few extra keystrokes.

This feature will turn you into a data filtering Ninja.

How to do it...

Just right-mouse-click on the field value that you want to filter based on, and then select the Filter By Selection option from the context menu.

The list page will then be filtered to just the records that match that field value.

How easy was that!

Use The Filter by Field To Search For Subsets Of Data Within Columns

Sometimes, you just want to search for all records within a list page that match some sort of criteria. If this is the whole value of a field then you can use the Filter By Selection feature, but if you want to be a little more flexible, and maybe search for subsets of data within the field, then there is a better way to do it by using the Filter By Field feature.

Now you can extract out the data like a surgeon rather than a butcher.

How to do it...

To quickly filter a column of data in a list page, just right-mouse-click on the field that you want to filter on, and then select the Filter by Field option from the sub-menu.

Alternatively, if your cursor is already on that field, then just press CTRL+F.

When the Filter dialog box is displayed, just type in the regular search expression that you want to filter with, and then click the OK button.

This will refresh the list page, and filter out the data based on the selection that you specified in the search.

That is too easy.

Use The Filter By Grid & Wild Cards To Create More Intricate Queries

Searching and filtering your records based on a field is pretty cool, but in order to hone in on just the right data that you need, you will probably want get a little more creative with your queries, by combining searches, filtering based on ranges, field formats, and value ranges. You will also probably want to filter based on multiple fields at once. Built into all of the list pages is a feature called Filter By Grid that allows you to do exactly that.

No data will be able to hide from you now.

How to do it...

To access the Filter By Grid feature on a list page, either click on the Filter By Grid icon in the title bar of the list page, or press CTRL+G.

This will enable a row at the top of the list page where you can add filters to any of the visible fields. All you need to do is start specifying what you want to search for.

You can use the * qualifier to indicate that any value before or after this point is valid, which is great for searching for records that all start, end, or have the same characters somewhere within the field.

You can use the ? expression to indicate that there must be a character in that spot – you don't care what it is though. This is a great way to select records that are of a certain length.

If you want to select a group of records within a range, then you can use the .. expression in the middle of the low and high filters. Note that the low and high values can also be wild carded as well.

If you want to combine multiple filters together, but not include any values in the middle, then you can append them together by adding a , between them. You can append as many queries together within a field as you like.

If you have a field that is numeric, then you can use the < and > expressions to select all of the data that is less than or greater than a certain value.

If you want to filter out certain data, then if you add a ! to the beginning of the filter, then you will be saying that you do not want that value. This is a great way to filter out data when there is less that you don't want than you do.

Finally, the most powerful feature of the Filter By Grid option is that you can filter multiple columns at once, creating super filters.

Using The Query Dialog To Create More Advanced Filters

There are a lot of different ways that you can filter out the information in Dynamics AX, but the most flexible one is the Query Dialog. You are probably familiar with this because it shows up a lot when you run updates and reports as the selection box. But you can also access it any time that you are on a list page by pressing CTRL+F3.

This allows you to quickly create custom filters on your data on that is both on the form, and also any additional fields that you may want to add to the query, without having to add additional fields to the form through the personalization. This makes it an incredibly useful way to refine your searches.

How to do it...

To access the Query Dialog, just press CTRL+F3 while you are on your list page.

When the dialog box is displayed, you will see all of the fields that are being filtered on by default are listed in the Range section.

If you click the Add button, then a new range entry will be created, and you can select from any field in the related tables to add as a search criteria.

After selecting a field to search on, you can also pull up a list of values for that field to add to your selection criteria.

When you have completed building your query, then you just press the OK button to return to your form.

Now you will see that the filter that you built through the Query Dialog has been applied to your form.

Setting Forms To Automatically Open In Edit Mode

There are those people that are casual users of Dynamics AX that look through the data and occasionally update it, and there are those that are always updating and tweaking the data in the system. If you are in the latter of the two groups, then you probably hate going into a form and having to click on the Edit button so that you can change the data. It may be one click, but if you are doing it thousands of times a day, then this quickly starts becoming a chore. Luckily there is a simple option that you can change that will make it so that every time you go into a form, it will automatically start in edit mode.

With all the spare time that you just got, what on earth will you do with yourself.

How to do it...

Click on the Files menu, select the Tools submenu, and then click on the Options menu item.

Within the General options, open up the Interface Options tab and change the Default Global View/Edit Mode to Edit.

When you are done, just click the Close button to exit the form.

Now whenever you open up a form, you will be in edit mode automatically and you don't even have to click on the Edit button in the ribbon bar.

Create Open Ended Filters By Using Ranges With No Beginning Or End

Everyone knows that you can use the ".." to search for ranges of records when you filter out your data, but it becomes even more useful when you skip either the beginning or end filter selection because then you can create a filter for everything before, or everything after a certain value.

It's like creating your own version of the Neverending (or Neverbegginning) story.

How to do it...

If you create a filter with a beginning value but no end value (like "400000..") then you will see everything from that record on in the system.

If you create a filter with a end value but no beginning value (like "..100010") then you will see everything up until that record on in the system.

Change The Default Language Within The Rich Client

Dynamics AX is truly a multi-lingual system, and switching the language that the client uses is just a matter of changing the an option.

It's like having your very own Babel Fish in your ear.

How to do it...

To change the language that your rich client uses, open up the Files menu select the Tools submenu, and then click on the Options menu item.

When the Options form is displayed, click on the Language dropdown field and you will be able to see all of the default languages that you can use for your client.

Select the language that you want to use and then close the Options form, and restart the client.

الآن يجب على العميل سوف تبدو مختلفة قليلاً.

لتغيير اللغة مرة أخرى، تفتح الملفات القائمة حدد القائمة الفرعية أدوات، ومن ثم انقر فوق عنصر القائمة "خيارات".

عندما يتم عرض النموذج خيارات، انقر فوق القائمة المنسدلة لحقل اللغة، وسوف تكون قادراً على مشاهدة كافة اللغات الافتراضية التي يمكنك استخدامها للعميل الخاص بك.

Ahora estarás en un idioma diferente.

Observe que todas las cajas de hecho y las partidas son cambiadas, así cuando taladra en los formularios.

Para volver a los ingleses, abra los archivos de menú Seleccione el submenú herramientas y luego haga clic en el menú de opciones.

Cambiar el idioma a tu idioma original quiere usar y luego cerrar el formulario de opciones y reiniciar el cliente.

Cambiar el idioma a tu idioma original quiere usar y luego cerrar el formulario de opciones y reiniciar el cliente.

Now we're back to the base language.

How cool is that!

If You Don't Like The Way Your Data Looks The Rename It

If you are as OCD about tidy data as I am, then you probably hate data that does not quite match up with everything else in the database. Maybe it's because you made a mistake in adding some data, or maybe you just want the data to look a little cleaner, we don't judge. Luckily you don't have to live with odd data within Dynamics AX, you can rename the records at any time and all of the related records will be renamed as well.

If it's good enough for Gordon Matthew Thomas Sumner then it's good enough for your data.

How to do it...

Start off by opening up the record that you want to rename.

Then right-mouse-click on the form and select the Record Info menu item

When the Record Information dialog box is displayed, click on the Rename button.

Then the Rename dialog box is displayed, just type in the new record key that you want to use and then click on the OK button.

If you are sure that you want to rename the record then click Yes when the dialog box is displayed.

Now when you return to the record you will notice that the record index has been changed.

Also, all of the associated records have been changed as well.

How cool is that.

Convert Any Record Into A Template

You may be familiar with the template capabilities that are available within the Released Products, but that isn't the only place that you can create templates. You can turn any record within Dynamics AX into a public or personal template that you can use to pre-populate fields saving you setup time, and also ensuring that all of the miscellaneous fields are configures just how you like them.

It's like having your own cookie cutter creator.

How to do it...

To do this, find the record that you want to use as a template.

Then right-mouse-click on the form and select the Record Info menu item.

When the Record Information dialog box is displayed, click on either the Company Accounts Template button if you want to make this template available to everyone, or the User Template button if you just want to create a template for your own personal use.

This will open up a Create Template dialog box where you just need to assign your template a Name and a Description and then click on the OK button.

Now when you create a new record, a Select A Template dialog box will be displayed where you can select which template you want to use as the foundation. All you need to do is select one and then click the OK button.

All of the information from the template will default in.

And all of those miscellaneous fields that takes the real setup time will be set up for you.

That should make life a lot easier.

FUNCTIONAL TRICKS

There is a lot that you can do functionally within Dynamics AX, but that should just be the starting point. There are a lot of features that are built into the application to support the core functions that allow you to take it to the next level. You just need to know what they are.

In this section we will show how you can use features like Workflow to streamline your approvals, Cases to manage incidents and issues, Print Management to automate document delivery, Portals for collaboration with partners, and also the Registration Forms to simplify production.

Topics Covered

- Add Approval Workflows to General Ledger Journals

- Use Cases To Track Customer Issues And Complaints

- Linking Knowledgebase Articles To Help Resolve Customer Complaints

- Manage Engineering Change Orders Through Cases

- Use Print Management To Automatically Email Documents To Customers & Vendors

- Use Print Management To Email Forms To All Customers By Business Purpose

- Create Collaboration Workspaces To Share Information

- Assign Workers To Projects Visually Using The Worker Reservation Screen

- Enter Sales Orders Over the Web Using The Sales Portal

- Let Your Vendors Enter Their Own Invoices Through The Vendor Portal

- Use The Job Registration Screen To Record Production Transactions

- Require Users To Review Production Documents Before Starting Jobs

- Applying Templates To Multiple Products At Once

- Update Product System Templates After They Have Been Created

- Rename Product Dimensions To Match Your Business

- Manage Your Product Costs By Product Variants

- Use Retail Category Attributes To Track Additional Product Characteristics

- Use Refilling Warehouses To Let MRP Suggest Replenishment Transfers

- Configure the Carrier Interface in Test Mode to Record Tracking Numbers Manually

- Configure Notes To Print On Standard Forms Like The Order Confirmation

- Assign Tasks To Other People Through Activities

- Creating a Mail Merges In Word From Campaign Target Lists

- Send Personalized Emails To Contacts Through Campaigns

- Creating Request For Quotations During The Requisitioning Process

- Track Skills And Education Against Everyone To Help Match People To Jobs

- Add Media To Questionnaires To Create Visual Training Exercises And Certifications

- Drilling Into AX Detail Directly From The Management Reporter Web Viewer

- Use Excel Worksheets To Make Entering Budgeting A Breeze

- Assign Shortcut Keys To POS Terminal Buttons

- Clock Workers In And Out Using Job Registration

- Change The Default Party Types From Organizations To Person

- Add Additional Email Purposes To Route Emails To Different Groups In An Organization

- Showing Contacts First Names Last and Last Names First

- Track Relationships Between Parties Through The Global Address Book

- Track Social Media Information Against Contacts

- Schedule Multiple Discussions At Once Through The Mass Creation Option

- Create Appointments In Outlook Directly From The Discussions

- Tally Packaging Quantities On Order Lines

- Generate Product Bar Code Labels Through Retail

- Quickly Update Prices For Released Products

- Mark Deleted Sales Orders As Voided To Track Lost Sales

- Block Users From Using Particular Journal Names By Making Them Private

- Use Workflows To Process AP Invoices Through Unattached Documents

- Enable Change Management On Purchase Orders To Track Changes

- Use Auto-Numbering Unless You Don't Feel Like It

- Split Your Number Sequences To Make Them Look Intelligent

- Use Pricing Models Within Configured Products To Calculate Prices Without A BOM

- Control Price Adjustments On Sales Orders

- Create Filtered Alerts To Sniff Out The Data You Really Want

- Declutter Customer Lists By Securing Them Through Address Books

- Set Default Parameter Values Into Posting Forms

Add Approval Workflows to General Ledger Journals

Workflows are available throughout Dynamics AX and are a great way to make sure that things don't get done by the right people, in a timely manner, and also provides a great way for people to see what they need to do because only the tasks that they need to worry about are assigned to them. An example of this is that you can create workflow approval processes on any of your GL Journal codes, ensuring that no-one posts journals without some sort of review.

Everyone seems a little bit intimidated by workflows – probably because they think that they require code, and that a developer needs to be involved to set them up - which can't be further from the truth. Configuring a workflow is as simple as laying out a diagram that describes what you want to do, and then just enabling it.

How to do it...

Before we start approving Journals, we need to create a workflow that we will use for the approval process. To do this, open up the General ledger workflows maintenance form from within the Setup group of the General Ledger area page.

Then click on the New button within the New group of the Workflow ribbon bar.

When the Create workflow dialog box is displayed, select the Ledger daily journal workflow item – since we are going to create a workflow for a journal type of Daily – and then click on the Create workflow button.

When the designer is displayed, drag over an Approve daily journal action over onto the canvas and link it to the Start and End nodes to create a simple approval workflow.

Some extra data will be required because you will need to assign a user(s) to the workflow approval step, and also will need to add some descriptions to the nodes, but if you look at the message pane, then it will direct you on what needs to be updated.

When you have done this, click on the Save and close button to save the workflow, and then activate it so that it is useable by Dynamics AX.

Now open up the Journal Names maintenance form from within the Journals folder of the Setup group of the General ledger area page.

Select the journal that you want to have controlled by the workflow process that you just designed, check the Approval workflow checkbox within the Approval workflow group, and then from the Workflow dropdown, select the workflow template that you just designed.

Now when you create a journal entry for the journal type that you enabled workflow on, the Post option will be disabled, and there will be a Submit button that you can click on to initiate the approval workflow.

The user that is responsible for approving the workflow will be notified either by a toast popup, an alert, or through email, depending on the notification options that you defined in the workflow that you designed.

The alert will take them directly to the record that they need to approve, and if they click on the Actions button, they are able to select the action that they want to apply to the journal. To allow the journal to be posted, all they need to do is select the Approve menu item.

Once the journal is approved, then the journal becomes postable, and only option that will be available to the user is the View history option.

This allows the user to see the complete history of the workflow approval, and also any comments that were made during the submission and approval process.

Use Cases To Track Customer Issues And Complaints

With the 2012 release of Dynamics AX, a new feature called "Cases" was introduced that allows you to create case files for just about anything that you care about within the business. This is not just a logging system though, you can attach files to the cases, record activities against the case, and also create workflows and business processes that track the progress of the case so that things don't slip through the cracks the way that the old fashioned paper method if prone to happen.

One way that you can use Cases is to track customer issues and complaints, because you can create cases directly from the main forms within Dynamics AX.

How to do it...

To create a new Case directly from the Customer List, click on the Case menu item within the New group of the General ribbon bar.

When the new case dialog box is displayed, select the type of Case from the Case category drop down tree. These are completely configurable by the user and can have as many levels and groupings as required.

Note: The Name will be automatically populated and linked back to the customer account because it was initiated with that record.

Fill in all of the other information about the case, including the Department that it should be associated with, the Employee responsible who will be assigned the case, and also and additional Description and Notes that you want to add to the case.

Now the case will be tracked within the system, and the users will be able to see all the reported incidents and filter by product, and customer.

There is also a lot more detail that you can track against the case, including an unlimited number of notes and comments.

Linking Knowledgebase Articles To Help Resolve Customer Complaints

There are no silver bullets when it comes to solving cases like customer complaints, but everyone usually has a library of common solutions that have worked in the past that they rely on as the first line of defense. Dynamics AX allows you to save away these documents as Knowledgebase Articles, and then link them to your case templates so that they are right at your fingertips every time a certain situation arises.

By doing this, you are always prepared to answer those tricky customer questions without having to rustle through your file folder for a particular document, or yell out over the cube wall to see if anyone else has come across the situation.

How to do it...

From within the Case Categories maintenance screen, select the Case Category that you would like to associate the Knowledgebase Articles to and click on the Related Knowledgebase Articles button in the menu bar.

When the Related Knowledgebase Articles form is displayed, you can add new knowledgebase articles that may help resolve the case from your library.

Once you have selected all of the knowledgebase articles that are appropriate, just close the dialog box and exit the Case Categories form.

Now when you create a case that has Knowledgebase articles related to it they will automatically show up in the Case maintenance form.

Clicking on any of the articles will open up the document for easy reference.

And also, you can track if you attempted to use the article, and also if it helped, so that you and others are able to see how useful the articles are.

Manage Engineering Change Orders Through Cases

With the CU7 release of Dynamics AX, a new Case Category type was added in called Product Change. The Cases functionality has also been added to the Product Management forms to allow you to create and associate cases to the Release Products, Routes, BOM's and BOM Lines. Additionally the Case Management has been enhanced to allow you to do Where-Used analysis on items, and add related products to the Product Change Request.

What a great way to manage Engineering Change Orders.

How to do it...

Before you start, you just need to go into the Case Categories maintenance form and add a new Case Category for your ECO request.

On the Released Products you will see a new button group within the Engineering ribbon bar for Product Change that allows you to create Product Change cases.

If you look at the Routes, you will also see a new Product Change menu item for creating Product Change Cases.

Finally, on the BOM's you will see a new Product Change menu item.

If you click on the Create Case from the Product Change dropdown menu, you will be able to create a new case and select from the Product Change Case Categories that you have defined.

You are then able to fill in the Description and Notes for the Product Change Case. When you have done that just click on the Create button to create the ECO.

Now your will have an ECO case to track the request.

If you want to associate an item with the Product Change Request, then you can select the line item from the BOM and click the Associate item with case menu item from the Product Change menu of the BOM lines.

You select the Product Change Request that you want to associate it with and then add any notes that you may want to pass along.

Now when you look at the Product Change Case, you will notice that the Product and Item have been associated with it.

If you select the Item, then you will be able to click on the Where Used Analysis button to find all related products and BOM's that utilize the product.

If you want to include all of the other BOM's into the Product Change Request, then all you need to do is click on the Associate all with the case button at the bottom of the screen.

Now when you return to the case, all of the other BOM's are recorded against the Product Change Request.

Since this is a Case then you also have all of the standard Case functionality at your fingertips, such as processes and workflows to help you manage the process. How cool is that.

Use Print Management To Automatically Email Documents To Customers & Vendors

The Print Management feature within Dynamics AX lets you override the default document delivery options by customer and vendor. One of the delivery methods is through email, all you need to do is specify the email address.

This allows you to have the system automatically email all of the common documents (i.e. sales order, purchase order, invoice etc.) without you having to generate the document, save it to your desktop, and then manually attach it to an email for the customer.

How to do it...

From the customers maintenance form, select the Print Management option from the Setup group of the General Ribbon bar

Step 2: Right-mouse-click on the document that you want to change to an e-mail delivery and select the Override option from the context menu.

Step 3: This will allow you to click on the arrow to the right of the Destination field settings, and select the Printer setup option

Step 4: When the Print destination settings dialog box is displayed, you can select the Email option, and specify the default email address to deliver the document to for that customer.

Now when you print out the order confirmation, select the Use print management destination and the defaults that are defined against the customer will be used and your document will be automatically emailed to the customer.

Without any cutting and pasting, the e-mail is delivered.

Use Print Management To Email Forms To All Customers By Business Purpose

The Print Management functions within Dynamics AX allow you to specify how and where forms and documents get sent, and you can configure it to automatically deliver documents like the Order Confirmations to customers by e-mail. With the CU7 release of Dynamics AX, a new feature was added that makes this even more useful, because you can set up global rules for the forms where you can tell it to send to particular e-mail purpose on the customer account rather than having to specify it by account.

By doing this you can have one Print Management rule, and then specify who receives the emails through the contact management on the customer record, making life so much easier.

How to do it...

Within your Customer maintenance form, open up the Contact Information tab, and from the More options menu button within the tab, select the Advanced menu item.

When the Edit Contact Information maintenance form is displayed, select the primary e-mail that you would like all documents to be emailed to and from the Purpose dropdown box, check the Business purpose and click the OK button.

When you have finished, click the OK button, and then exit out of the Customer maintenance form.

Select the Form Setup menu item from within the Forms folder of the Setup group of the Accounts Receivable area page.

When the Form Setup dialog box is displayed, click on the Print Management button to the right of the form on the General tab group.

When the Print Management Setup dialog box is displayed, select the form that you would like to automatically send based on the contact information on the customer record, and then click on the > button to the far right of the Destination field.

Then click on the Printer Setup menu item.

When the Print Destination Settings dialog box is displayed, click on the Edit menu button to the right of the To field.

This will open up the Assign Email Address form. Click on the Customer Purpose dropdown box.

Then select the default Purpose that you want to select from the Customer account whenever the document is emailed.

To tidy things up, add a Subject for the e-mail and then click the OK button to save the configuration.

Now select a Sales Order, and create a Sales Order Confirmation.

When the Confirm Sales Order dialog box is displayed, make sure that you select the Print Confirmation and also the Use Print Management Destination so that it will use the overriding default setup for print management, and then click on the OK button.

This will create an e-mail message to the email account on the Customer that is has the same Purpose, and attach the Order Confirmation document to it, all in one fell swoop.

Create Collaboration Workspaces To Share Information

There are times when multiple people are working on a project and you need a place to share all of the common documents, and also a place where everyone is able to collaborate and add their input. Dynamics AX has an inbuilt feature that is designed just to allow that called Collaboration Workspaces, which are linked to a number of the functions such as Projects, Campaigns, Cases etc. allowing you from the record to create a SharePoint workspace that everyone is able to access and collaborate through.

Not only is this much better than the usual way of doing this which is usually through some sort of shared network folder, or even worse, a folder on someone's desktop, it is more secure, and also gives you the ability to use all of the functions within SharePoint to really share information.

All you need to do is create the workspace and you are up and going.

How to do it...

From the Projects master form, click on the Collaboration workspace menu button from the Setup group of the Project ribbon bar, and select the Create collaboration workspace option.

When the Create collaboration workspace dialog box is displayed, you can just accept the defaults, and click on the OK button to create the workspace.

Note: You can change the default template that is chosen for you though, if you have different pre-configured workspace formats that you use for different scenarios.

Once this is done, you will notice that there are now linked workspaces in the Collaboration workspaces tab of the form.

If you click on the links that were assigned, you will be taken to the collaboration workspace where you can start filing away all of the project information.

Assign Workers To Projects Visually Using The Worker Reservation Screen

Scheduling resources for projects can be difficult, especially if you have a large group of workers that you are trying to manage. Luckily for you all, Dynamics AX has a feature for visually seeing all of your workers available capacity, and also for quickly allocating workers to projects.

Now you can stop relying on Outlook being up to date, and schedule the way that you should done.

How to do it...

Open up your project and from within the Project and Scheduling group, click on the Add Roles menu button.

When the Add roles to project selection box is displayed, select a Role Template and then click on the OK button.

When the Worker Reservation form is displayed, you will be able to see all of the workers that are available for the project, also with the capacity that's available.

If you mark a worker, then all available capacity will be assigned to the project.

You can also click on any available capacity of the worker to mark them as assigned for the selected periods.

When you have done that, click on the Hard Book button to allocate the resources to the project.

Even though you initially created a selection for one worker within the project, if you select multiple workers then the will be added to the project as well.

Now when you return to the project, you will see that the workers have been assigned as resources.

Enter Sales Orders Over the Web Using The Sales Portal

Dynamics AX includes a number of web based portals that are designed to allow you to access almost all of the same information that is available within the traditional rick client through a much thinner interface. One of the portals is a sales portal that allows you to look up customer information, record activities against the customers and even place orders through the web that are then immediately available for everyone regardless of how they are accessing the system.

This is a great way for salespeople to quickly access information from Dynamics AX on their laptops, or even through their tablets, because all they need is a connection to the Enterprise Portal site and a web browser.

How to do it...

To see all of the orders through the web, just open up the Sales Portal from within the Enterprise Portal, and click on the Sales Orders menu item within the Common menu group on the left.

To place a new order, the user just needs to click on the Sales Order button within the New group of the Sales order ribbon bar.

When the New sales order dialog box is displayed, you can enter in all of the header information for the order such as the Customer account, the Contact for the order, and also the sourcing information for the sales order.

Within the Lines group, if you click on the Add line button within the menu bar, it will allow you to enter in all of the line information such as the Item number, quantity, and also all of the default pricing information will be automatically calculated for you.

Also other functionality such as product configuration are built into the sales portal as well.

Once the order is saved through the Sales Portal, it is immediately available to everyone through the rich client.

Let Your Vendors Enter Their Own Invoices Through The Vendor Portal

If you want to streamline part of the Accounts Payables processing, why not let your vendors post their invoices themselves through the Vendor Portal rather than with a stamp through the USPS. Through the portal they are able to enter in all of the billing information and line details, and also attach any supporting information as document attachments that will then show up within the Payables area page as pending invoices. The invoice then just needs to be reviewed and approved and it will be ready for payment.

You will become more efficient, because you don't have to re-key in invoice details as they arrive in the paper format, and also the vendors should be happier because you will be able to pay them sooner because there isn't any lag between the invoice being posted and it being available for review for the payables group. Everyone's a winner.

How to do it...

The vendor just needs to log into the Vendor Portal, and select the Vendor Invoices page from the Orders group, and then click on the Invoice button within the New group of the Invoice ribbon bar.

Then a New Invoice dialog box will be displayed into which they just specify the invoice number in the Number field, and add a brief description in the Vendor description field.

When they have done that they can click on the Create button to create the new invoice.

When the Edit Invoice window is displayed, they can enter in the invoice detailed, including the invoice lines, and when they are finished, click on the Save and close button within the Commit group of the Edit ribbon bar.

When they return to the Vendor invoices page they will see the new invoice that they had entered.

Within Dynamics AX, you will be able to see all of the pending invoices by clicking on the Pending Invoices menu item within the Vendor Invoices folder of the Common group of the Accounts Payable area page.

Clicking on the pending invoice will show all of the payables people the same details that he vendor typed in themselves, and they just need to approve it to make it a valid invoice.

Use The Job Registration Screen To Record Production Transactions

Posting time and materials to production jobs does not have to be a manual, or an after the fact process. Dynamics AX has a featured called Job Registration that allows you to report all of your manufacturing actions in real time through a simple to use touch screen. It tracks all of the material issues in real time, and also tracks who is performing the transaction as well, giving you greater visibility of who is working.

No more hand written job sheets that get updated the next day.

How to do it...

Click on the Job Registration menu item within the Manufacturing Execution folder of the Periodic group within the Production Control area page.

When the Job Registration touch screen is displayed, type in your Employee ID and Password and then click on the Login button.

When the Select Resource and Action dialog box is displayed, select the Resource that you want to report against, and then click on the Job Registration action.

If this is the first action that you have performed then it will automatically clock you in.

When the Job Registration touchscreen appears you will be able to see all of the active jobs.

If you click on the Start Jobs button within the Job List group of the Manage Activities ribbon bar, then your will start the processing of the route step.

If you click on the Feedback button within the Report Feedback group of the Manage Activities ribbon bar, you will be able to report quantities, and also finish the route steps.

You can stop working at any time by clicking on the Clock Out button within the Time and Attendance Registration group on the Manage Activities ribbon bar which will also post your time against the production job.

If you look at the Production Journals that are associated with the production order all of your transactions that you reported against the production job through the Job Registration screen will be posted for you.

How easy is that.

Require Users To Review Production Documents Before Starting Jobs

Attaching process specifications, and safety instructions to Bills Of Material, Jobs, or Process Specs a great feature, if they are not read by the workers when they are performing the jobs, then they don't do anyone any good. Luckily, Dynamics AX has a feature within the Production module that allows you to specify that certain documents must be reviewed before starting jobs.

Now no-one can plead ignorance about new processes or procedures.

How to do it...

Make sure that you have some document types configured for the types of documents that you are going to attach to your BOMs.

Click on the Document Groups menu item within the Setup group of the Production Control area page.

When the Document Groups maintenance form is displayed, click on the New button within the menu bar to create a new record, and then assign your new Document Group an ID and a Description.

To add a new type of document that needs to be reviewed, click on the Add menu button within the Document Types menu bar, and select the Document Type from the list of types that you have configured.

If you want the document to be reviewed by the user before starting the manufacturing job, then check the Required Reading check box.

If you only need them to review it when they start the job, and not every time that they check in to the job, then click on the Required Once check box.

If you want certain users to review the document then click the Add button within the Members group, and add any of the workers that you like.

The next step is to associate your document with the BOM.

Open up the BOM that you want to attach the document for review, click on the Attachment icon (which may be in the bottom left of the status bar) and then link your document to it.

Now when you start any job, then you will be notified that you need to review the document that you attached to the BOM.

By clicking on the Open Documents button, Dynamics AX will open up all of the documents that you have required the users to review.

Applying Templates To Multiple Products At Once

Product templates are a great timesaver, because they allow you to set up one product, save it's configuration as a template record, and then use it to create new records with those defaults, or apply it to existing records to update the key fields.

If you are updating existing records, you don't have to do them one at a time though, if you select multiple product records, then you can apply the same template to them all in one fell swoop, saving you a lot of time, especially during the data setup phase.

How to do it...

Start off by selecting the product that you want to use as the template and then click on the Template button within the New group of the Product ribbon bar to see the template options. Select the Create personal template option.

When the Create template dialog box is displayed, give your template a Name and Description and then click the OK button.

Now return to the Release Products grid view and select all of the products that you want to apply the template to and click on the Apply template button within the Maintain group of the Product ribbon bar.

Select your template that you just created, and then click on the OK button.

Now all of the products that you applied the templates to will be configured the same way.

Update Product System Templates After They Have Been Created

Product templates are a great time saver because they allow you to use an existing product as a example of how to set up other products, making product setup more of a cookie cutter production line rather than a laborious hand crafting of each record. But as your business changes, you will probably find that you want to update your product templates so that you don't have to continually tweak fields here and there that have changed over time, or maybe you want to remove templates that are now obsolete so that the users don't see them when they are creating new product records.

Don't worry, you can do this directly through the Record Template maintenance form within the Home Area page.

How to do it...

Select the Record Templates menu item from within the Setup group of the Home area page.

When the Record templates maintenance form is displayed, you will be able to see all of the records that have templates associated with them. In this case we just have templates for the Items.

If you click on the Templates tab you will be able to see all of the system templates that you have defined. To change the template, click on the Edit button on the right.

This will open up the Released product that you selected to be the product template, and you can make changes to the key information. Once you have updated the record, click the Close button, and the next time you create a product from that template it will use the new defaults that you defined.

Rename Product Dimensions To Match Your Business

Product Dimensions within Dynamics AX are great because they give you four extra elements that you can use to segregate out all of your products, and you can start reducing the number of base product codes that you use. By default the main three dimensions are named Size, Color, and Style, but if you think of your product dimensions in different terms, don't disregard this feature, because you can rename them to be whatever you like.

Now you can build your product dimensions however you like.

How to do it...

Click on the Product Dimension Groups menu item within the Dimension Groups folder of the Setup group within the Product Information Management area page.

When the Product Dimension Groups maintenance form is displayed, click on any of the records, and then select the Dimension that you want to repurpose. If the dimension is enabled, then the Rename button will become enabled, and you can click on it.

This will open up the Rename Product Dimension Size dialog box. All of the standard text strings will be shown for the dimension.

All you need to do is update the standard messages to match the new dimension that you want to track against the products. When you have updated the 36 message files, just click on the OK button to update the dimension.

When you return to the Product Dimension Groups maintenance form you should notice that your dimension now uses the new naming convention that you set up.

Now when you maintain the valid product dimension values, it will have a new name.

Also, when you look at the dimension within the Released Product maintenance form, it will use the new naming convention.

Even the Inventory screens will be changed.

How cool is that!

Manage Your Product Costs By Product Variants

The Product Dimensions are great because they allow you to break out your products into multiple variants based on the rules that you put in place for the product. If those variations are priced and costed differently, then don't worry, there is a quick and easy way to enable costing by variation within Dynamics AX, enabling you to track everything at the product level, but treat them differently based on their configuration.

All products are equal, just some are more equal than others.

How to do it...

Open up the Released Product record and expand the Manage Costs tab group.

Then check the Use Cost Price By Variant check box.

Now when you look at the costs for your Released Product, you will see that the costs are now broken out by the different product variation.

Use Retail Category Attributes To Track Additional Product Characteristics

If you need to track additional characteristics and fields against a product record, you don't have to resort to making a coding change to Dynamics AX. You can add an unlimited number to additional Attributes to a Released Product through the Retail Categories functionality.

Please stop the unnecessary creation of new fields.

How to do it...

First we need to configure the Attribute Types that we will be using. To do this, click on the Attribute Types menu item within the Attributes folder of the Setup group within the Product Information Management area page.

Within the Attribute Types maintenance form, add a new record for each of the different types that you will be using for your attributes.

The next step is to configure the Attributes themselves that we will be using. To do this, click on the Attributes menu item within the Attributes folder of the Setup group within the Product Information Management area page.

Within the Attributes maintenance form, add a new record for each of the different attribute that you want to track against the products and then link them to the Attribute Type that they will be using.

Now we need to configure an Attributes Group that will be used to reference all of the Attributes that we will be using. To do this, click on the Attribute Groups menu item within the Attributes folder of the Setup group within the Product Information Management area page.

Within the Attribute Groups maintenance form, add a new record for an attribute group and then add all of the Attributes that you want to use within that group.

Finally we need to associate the Attribute Group to a Retail Product Hierarchy so that it will default in the Attributes against a product. To do this, click on the Retail Product Hierarchy menu item within the Category Hierarchy folder of the Setup group within the Retail area page.

When the Retail Product Hierarchy maintenance form is displayed, click on the node in the hierarchy that you want to inherit the attributes, and add the Attribute Group to the Product Attribute Groups tab.

If you look at the values within the Category Attribute Values tab, then all of the attributes that you assigned to the group will show up there.

To enable the Attributes against a product all you need to do is have the product assigned to the Retail Category Hierarchy that you configured the Attribute Group against. To do this open up the Released Product and click on the Product Categories menu button within the Setup group of the Product ribbon bar.

If the Retail category is not associated with the product then just click on the New button in the menu bar to create a new record, and then link the product to the Retail Category.

Now when you open up the product and click on the Product Attributes menu button within the Setup group of the Product ribbon bar, you will see all of the attributes are listed and you can maintain the values.

What a great way to track additional field values against a product without any code.

Use Refilling Warehouses To Let MRP Suggest Replenishment Transfers

Dynamics AX allows you to specify warehouses that are designated to refill other warehouses. This feature is really useful because it will make MRP top up the stock within the child warehouses through transfers rather than a purchase order, and then plan to purchase more product at the refilling warehouse to cover the demand. There is also no limit to the number of levels that you can have, so smaller retail locations can be refilled from area distribution centers, which could be replenished from a central production of receiving center.

This makes your purchasing a lot more centralized and stops you from nickel and diming your suppliers with small orders from each location.

How to do it...

To set up the warehouse refilling policies, just click on the Warehouses link within the Inventory Breakdown folder of the Setup group within the Inventory and Warehouse Management area page.

In this example our first warehouse is the centralized purchasing location, so don't check the Refilling option within the Master Planning tab.

This next warehouse is refilled from the distribution center, so check the Refilling option and set the Main Warehouse to be the parent distribution center warehouse.

For the final warehouse we will also check the Refilling option but set the Main Warehouse to be the local distribution warehouse.

Now when you run your MRP, if you have demand at the child warehouse, then planning will create a transfer from the local distribution center to satisfy it, and that in turn will be replenished from the main warehouse through a transfer as well.

Now you just have to organize for the carriers and you are done.

Configure the Carrier Interface in Test Mode to Record Tracking Numbers Manually

If you want to track parcel shipment tracking numbers within Dynamics AX, but have not got the volume of orders to justify installing the FedEx, or UPS software, then don't worry. You can track this information manually by turning on the Carrier Interfaces, but configuring them to run in test mode.

Configured this way, you will be asked to enter in the tracking information whenever the Packing Slip is created.

How to do it...

Click on the Carrier Interface menu item within the Shipping Carrier folder of the Setup group within the Inventory and Warehouse Management area page.

When the Carrier Interface maintenance form is displayed, check the Enabled and Test Mode check boxes for the FedEx and UPS Carrier Interface ID's.

Next, click on the Carrier Company menu item within the Shipping Carrier folder of the Setup group within the Inventory and Warehouse Management area page.

When the Carrier Company maintenance form is displayed, add two new records for FedEx, and UPS.

Note: If you want to configure the tracking number URL links, then here they are:

http://www.fedex.com/Tracking?ascend_header&clienttype=dotc
om&cntry_code=us&language=english&trackingnumbers=%1

http://wwwapps.ups.com/WebTracking/processInputRequest?HT
MLVersion=5.0&loc=en_US&tracknum=%1

Now, click on the Carrier IDs menu item within the Shipping
Carrier folder of the Setup group within the Inventory and
Warehouse Management area page.

When the Carrier IDs maintenance form is displayed, add records
for each of the services that you want to use for each carrier.

Finally, click on the Modes of Delivery menu item within the
Distribution folder of the Setup group within the Sales and
Marketing area page.

When the Modes of Delivery maintenance form is displayed, you
can either create new records for the Carrier Service ID's that you
created, or associate them with existing Modes of Delivery to
make them the default.

Now when you create a Sales Order that has a Mode of Delivery
that has a Carrier Interface associated with it, since this is in test
mode, it will ask you to fill in all of the shipping information by
hand.

You can then inquire on the Packing Slip Journal at any time and
see all of the carrier tracking information.

Also, if you want more detailed information on the tracking
details for the shipment, click on the Inquiries menu button within
the Overview tab of the Packing Slip Journal inquiry form, and
select the Carrier Transaction Information option.

This will show you all of the Tracking Information, and also give
you a link to the carriers web tracking portal.

Configure Notes To Print On Standard Forms Like The Order Confirmation

The forms standard forms like the Order Confirmation are a lot more dynamic than you may think. If you have standard notes that you want to include on every document, or if you need to add record specific notes to the header of the lines then they can be configured to pick up the document attachment notes all without a single line of code.

No more sticky notes on your documents.

How to do it...

Before we start we need to make sure that the notes are configured to show on the standard documents within Dynamics AX. In order to do this, click on the Form Setup menu item within the Forms folder of the Setup group within the Accounts Receivable area page

When the Form Setup options are displayed, click on the form that you want to include the notes on.

From the dropdown box for the Include documents on sheets field select the locations that you would like the notes to display on.

From the dropdown box for the Include documents of type field select the type of note that you would like to display on. You can create additional document types if you like to further differentiate the notes.

When you have done that, just click on the Close button to exit out of the form.

To setup standard notes that display on the documents, click on the Form Notes menu item within the Forms folder of the Setup group within the Accounts Receivable area page.

When the Form Notes maintenance form is displayed, you can select the form that you want to add the standard verbiage to and then add the text to the Form Note memo box.

When you have done that, just click on the Close button to exit out of the form.

To add a note to the header of the order, click on the Attachments menu button within the Attachments group of the Sales Order tab of the Sales Order record.

When the Document Handling dialog box is displayed, add a new note with the same Type that you specified in the form setup, add the notes into the body of the attachment, and then set the Restriction field to External.

When you have done that, just click on the Close button to exit out of the form.

To add a note to the order line, click on the Sales Order Lines menu within the Sales Order Lines group and select the Attachments menu item.

Just as with the header notes, when the Document Handling dialog box is displayed, add a new note with the same Type that you specified in the form setup, add the notes into the body of the attachment, and then set the Restriction field to External.

Note also that you can add as many notes as you like to the line (or header).

When you have done that, just click on the Close button to exit out of the form.

Now when you print out the Order Confirmation, all of your notes will be picked up and printed.

Rock on!

Assign Tasks To Other People Through Activities

You don't have to have all of the CRM functions enabled within Dynamics AX in order to take advantage of some of the features that it offers. You can use features like Activities without any additional setup, which allows you to create appointments, notes, and also tasks.

These activities don't even have to be for you either. If you want to send someone a gentle reminder, then you can create a task, and assign it to anyone in the organization. The task will then show up on their activity list, and also pop up as a reminder in Outlook (if you have the synchronization enabled).

How to do it...

You will usually find the Activities menu button on the General ribbon bar of most of the key record maintenance forms. If you expand the menu you will see all of the different types of Activities that you can track. To create a task, just click on the New task menu item.

You can give your task a Purpose, a Description, and assign it to a another user by changing the Responsible field.

The users are able to see all of the tasks that they have been assigned by opening up the My Activities for from the Activities folder of the Common group of the Home area page.

Creating a Mail Merges In Word From Campaign Target Lists

Sometimes you need to create a more traditional paper mailing for your campaigns, but that doesn't mean that you need to jump through a lot of hoops in order to get it done. The Campaigns function within Dynamics AX has the ability to create mail merge exports directly from the application that can then be married up to Word mail merge templates. Once you have set this up, your standard mailings are just a matter of clicking a couple of buttons.

Let's keep the USPS in business people.

How to do it...

First we need to create a mail merge source file. To do this open up your Campaign with all of the targets selected, and click on the Mail Merge File menu button within the Create group of the Targets tab.

When the Mailing File dialog box is displayed, specify a file path for a .csv file that you will be using to store all of your mail merge data within, and then click the OK button.

When you open up the .csv file, you will see that all of the contact information for the Campaign Targets will be there and formatted for you.

Now we will want to create a mail merge template that we will use as the basis for our campaign mail merge. To do this, open up Word, and select the Use an Existing List menu item from the Select Recipients button within the Create Mail Merge group of the MAILINGS ribbon bar.

Then select the mail merge file that was created in the previous step.

When the File Conversion dialog box is displayed, just select the Other Encodings option, and click the OK button.

To check that the file has been read correctly, click on the Edit Recipient List button within the Start Mail Merge group of the MAILINGS ribbon bar and you should be able to see all of the records that were transferred from the campaign.

If this is the first time that you are doing this, then you may also have to click on the Match Fields button within the Write & Insert Fields group of the MAILINGS ribbon bar and make sure that all of the fields from the campaign match up to the ones that Word are expecting.

Now all you need to do is select the fields from the Insert Merge Fields button within the Write & Insert Fields group of the MAILINGS ribbon bar and add them to the document.

After you have created your mailing, save the template mail merge document.

To perform the mail merge, click on the Mail Merge File button within the Broadcast group of the Targets ribbon bar of the Campaign maintenance form.

This will show you a list of all your extracts for the Campaign. Find the extract that you want to use and then paste in the path of the Word template mail merge file that you created.

To link the data with the template, just click on the Template File button.

This will open up the template file and you can click on the Edit Individual Documents link under the Finish & Merge button within the Finish group of the MAILINGS ribbon bar.

This will create all of your merged files for you incorporating all of the data from the campaign.

Rock On!

Send Personalized Emails To Contacts Through Campaigns

The Campaigns feature within Dynamics AX is a great way to plan & manage marketing projects, but it is also a great way to market to your prospects and customers as well. Once you create your campaign, you can broadcast it through traditional methods like snail mail, or through e-mail blasts with the click of the button.

Getting the word out has never been so easy.

How to do it...

Start off by creating a campaign, and then assigning your target recipients to it.

Next, open up the Email Broadcast tab within the Campaign, and select a email template Name.

If you don't have an e-mail template created, then just create a new one that has a Subject and a Body. Remember that you can use the email template placeholders to add in personal information from the Contact and Campaign record.

Once you have selected the Email Template the Subject and E-mail Text will populate themselves.

To send an e-mail blast to all of the targets within your Campaign just click on the Web Responses menu item within the Broadcast group of the Targets ribbon bar.

When you check your outbox, then you will see all of the personalized emails.

How easy is that!

Creating Request For Quotations During The Requisitioning Process

The good thing about requisitions is that the users are able to ask for almost anything, although when they ask for something that you have never purchased before, someone has to source it. Dynamics AX makes this a lot easier, because you are able to create a Request For Quotation for any of the requisitioned lines directly from the Requisition itself that then automatically updates the requisition lines when a vendor quote has been approved.

No more off line quoting and manually tracking vendor quotes.

How to do it...

To create a Request For Quotation from a Requisition, click on the Request For Quotation button within the New group of the Purchase Requisition ribbon bar of the Purchase Requisitions form when it is assigned to you.

This will open up a dialog box where you can select the lines that you want to submit for Request For Quote. After selecting all the lines that you want to convert to a RFQ click on the OK button to exit from the form.

When you open up the Request For Quotations form, you will now see that a new Request For Quotation has been created with all of the lines from the requisition already populated for you.

Just add the vendors that you want to request the quotation from within the Vendor tab and then click on the Send button within the Processing group of the Quotation ribbon bar.

Then it's a matter of waiting for the Vendor to respond to your Request For Quotation (hopefully they will be able to use the on-line Vendor Portal) and if you want to use the quoted values in your Requisition, just click on the Accept button within the Process group of the Reply ribbon bar.

When you return to the Requisition, the quoted values from the Request For Quotation will be automatically updated within the Requisition Lines and also the Vendor will be assigned as well.

All you need to do now is approve the Requisition and then convert it to a Purchase Order.

How easy is that.

Track Skills And Education Against Everyone To Help Match People To Jobs

If you are always searching for people with certain job skills or education for those more specialized jobs, then why not track the Skills and Education levels Dynamics AX. You can track this personal information not only against employees and workers, but also any contact that you have within the system. Then you can use the Skill Mapping functions to find matches.

Consider this tool your own personal recruiter.

How to do it...

In order to search for people based on their skills and education, you need to first make sure that you are tracking that information.

To update the Education levels against Employees and Workers, open up the record, select the Competencies and Development tab, and then click on the Education link within the Competencies group.

This will allow you to add all of the Education levels that are associated with the worker.

You can also track the Education and Skill levels against Applicants within the HR module as well. To do this, open up the Applicant record, and then click on the Education button within the Competencies group of the Applicant ribbon bar.

When the Education maintenance form is displayed, you can add any Education details you like against the Applicant.

Finally, if you want to even track the Skills and Education against contacts (in essence every contact in Dynamics AX) then just open up the Contact record and click on the Education button within the Competencies group of the Competencies tab.

When the Education maintenance form is displayed, you can add any Education details you like against the Contact as well.

A quick way to search for people that have certain skills, click on the Skill Mapping menu item within the Skills folder of the Periodic group within the Human Resources area page.

When the Skill Mapping dialog box is displayed, set the Selection criteria to match the Skills and Education that you need, and then click on the OK button.

This will return a list of Workers, Contacts and Applicants that match your search.

How cool is that!

Add Media To Questionnaires To Create Visual Training Exercises And Certifications

Questionnaires are a great way within Dynamics AX to gather information, but you are not just limited to using text in them. There is an option that also allows you to associate media files with individual questions that are showed in conjunction with the questions.

This allows you to create visual training and testing Questionnaires that you can assign to employees to complete if you have training and certification requirements.

How to do it...

Select the Questions menu item from within the Design subfolder of the Questionnaires folder in the Common group of the Home area page.

When the Questions maintenance form is displayed, click on the New button in the menu bar to create a new question.

Set the Input Type to Checkbox, and give your question some Instructions and also the Text prompt.

Then click on the Media button in the menu bar.

When the Media dialog box is displayed, click on the Add button in the menu bar to associate some media to the question.

When the Create/update medium dialog box is displayed, specify the Filename and also the Width and Height and then click on the OK button.

When you return to the Media dialog box you should be able to see the animation that you added.

Repeat the addition of the Question, but this time, specify the question that you want associated with the video.

When you have finished, just click on the Close button to exit from the form.

Next, select the Questionnaires menu item from within the Design subfolder of the Questionnaires folder in the Common group of the Home area page.

When the Questionnaires maintenance form is displayed, click on the New button in the menu bar to create a new questionnaire.

Assign your Questionnaire a name and a Description.

Now click on the Questions button on the menu bar, and select the Questions menu item.

When the Questions maintenance form is displayed, click the New button in the menu bar to add a new question.

From the Question dropdown, select the first question that you just added.

Repeat the process again for the second question, and then click the close button to exit from the form, and return to the main menu.

To test the Questionnaire, select the Complete a questionnaires menu item from within the Questionnaires folder in the Common group of the Home area page.

Select the Questionnaire and click the Start button in the menu bar.

You will now see the first question, along with the animated media. After you have viewed it, just click on the Forward button to move to the next question.

Now you have to answer the test question, and you can click End when you are finished.

Drilling Into AX Detail Directly From The Management Reporter Web Viewer

If you use Management Reporter, then you probably already know that you can drill into the Dynamics AX transactions directly from the Windows based report viewer. You can also do the same through the web based viewer, which is so much cooler.

Now you can browse through your financial reports on your Surface knowing that you can always get back to your detail at any time.

How to do it...

In the Management Reporter web client, select the line item that you want to drill into.

A small triangle will appear in the top left hand corner of the cell that will open up a link to Open in Microsoft Dynamics which you can click on.

The Voucher Transactions form will the open within the Dynamics AX client allowing you to drill into the source data.

Use Excel Worksheets To Make Entering Budgeting A Breeze

At first glance, entering in all of your budgets within Dynamics AX may seem like a daunting prospect, because it looks like you need to break all of your budget entries out by account, and then by period. But it's not really the case. You can link all of your budget with Excel templates that you can then use to make the entry an extremely simple task.

Budgeting within Dynamics AX does not have to be a painful process.

How to do it...

When you are assigned a budget to update, rather than entering in the budget line by line, and period by period, just click on the Worksheet button within the Supplemental group of the Budget Plan ribbon bar.

This will open up the budget entry template within Excel, and populate it with all of your budget detail.

All you have to do now is update all of the budgets by account and period, and then click on the Publish All option of the Publish menu button within the Update group of the Dynamics AX ribbon bar.

Now when you return to your budget detail within Dynamics AX, you will see that it has added records for you for all of the new budget entry records, and updated all of the budget figures with the values that you entered in the worksheet.

Also, you can always return to the worksheet by clicking on it within the Budget Plan Documents fact box.

How cool is that!

Assign Shortcut Keys To POS Terminal Buttons

Even through the Point Of Sale screens that are available for Dynamics AX are designed to be poked and prodded through touchscreens, if you are a keyboard jockey, then you may want to be able to use shortcut keys to get around to speed things up a little. If you don't have any shortcuts already defined, then you can easily do this directly within the POS application.

Now you will be able to zip around within the POS screens faster than Neo in The Matrix.

How to do it...

To add a shortcut key to any button on the POS screen, just right-mouse-click on it and select the Button Properties option.

When the Configure Button form is displayed, just change the Text on Button field to include a description that has an "&" before the letter that you want to use as the shortcut key.

When you are done then just click the OK button.

In this example, I can start off on the main form of the POS Register, and then press ALT-V.

And I will be taken straight into the Voids and Returns sub-menu.

Clock Workers In And Out Using Job Registration

The Job Registration screens within the Production Management area gives you a great way to update your production jobs through touchscreens, but it can also be used for a lot of other functions as well including time clock checking in and out.

Workers just need to swipe their badge and the clock starts ticking.

How to do it...

The first step is to configure the workers so that they are allowed to use the Registration screens, and enable the clocking in feature. To do this, click on the Workers menu item within the Workers folder of the Common group of the Human Resources area page.

Select the worker (or workers) that you want to enable for clocking in and out, and then click on the Activate on Registration Terminals button within the Maintain group of the Time Registration ribbon bar.

When the Create Time Registration Worker dialog box is displayed, configure all of the required groups and profile defaults and then select the Check In or Out Configuration profile.

Note: if you only want the user to check in and out, then check the Use Timecard option.

When you are done, just click the Close button to exit from the form.

One other configuration that you will need to perform is to assign a Password to the Worker. To do this, just open up the Worker record, select the Employment group, and you will find the Password field within the Time Registration tab group.

Now you can click on the Job Registration menu item within the Manufacturing Execution folder of the Periodic group within the Production Control area page.

This will open up the Job Registration form where the user is able to type in their ID (or scan their badge) and then type in their password.

If they are a Time Registration enabled worker then it will check them in.

The next time that they log in, it will check them out.

Also, to see all of the check ins and outs, all you need to do is click on the Registration History menu item within the Registration folder of the Inquiries group within the Production Control area page.

This will show you everyone's records, and all of the check in and out time stamps.

How cool is that.

Change The Default Party Types From Organizations To Person

When you create a new Party record like a Customer, Vendor, Prospect etc. The default Record Type that is used is Organization, which is OK if you are always working with companies. But if you are working with people as your main account, then every time you create the record, you need to change the Record Type to Person. This soon becomes a little annoying.

Rather than torture yourself, just change the default Record Type for those Parties to Person and life will be good again.

How to do it...

To do this, click on the Global Address Book Parameters menu item within the Global Address Book folder of the Setup group within the Organization Administration area page.

Within the General group you will see the field group titled Select default record types for entities, where you can change the default type from Organization to Person.

Just change the records that you don't want to be Organizations by default to Persons and then click the Close button.

Now when you create a Party record that you changed the type for it will automatically default in as Person.

Add Additional Email Purposes To Route Emails To Different Groups In An Organization

The Print Management function within Dynamics AX is great, and got even better with the CU7 release of R2 when the ability to tokenize your e-mail destinations were added. But by default, there are only a handful of ways that you can segregate out your contact details, and if you have a customer that has multiple departments and you need to send out emails to different people depending on the purpose, it is still a little restrictive. Don't worry though, you can create your own new Business Purpose codes within Dynamics AX and then use them within the Print Management to route different documents to different addresses.

Rain or shine, that e-mail will now get to the right person.

How to do it...

Click on the Address and Contact Information Purpose menu item within the Global Address Book folder of the Setup group within the Organization Administration area page.

When the Address and Contact Information Purpose maintenance form is displayed, click on the New button within the menu bar to create a new record.

Assign your record a Purpose code, and a Description and then check the Postal Address checkbox if you want this to apply to the postal addresses, and check the Contact Information checkbox if you want this purpose to apply to emails and phone numbers.

Now when you open up your contact details you will see your new Purpose shows up in the list, and you can mark your e-mails to be associated with it.

Now when you configure your Print Management you will be able to select your Purpose from the list when you assign the emails using a token.

And from now on when you print out the report and have it automatically emailed, it will look for the contact details that match the purpose.

Invoices can go to one account, and confirmations can go to another.

Showing Contacts First Names Last and Last Names First

The order in which contacts names are displayed is a divisive debate that has been raging ever since there have been address books. Should the first name come first, or the last name? Microsoft Dynamics AX has made it's stand by showing the first name first, but if you are a firm believer that the last name is king, then don't worry, with a quick parameter change you can change the way that all of the contact names are displayed.

Now everyone is able to live in peace and harmony with their contact lists ordered how they like.

How to do it...

Initially all of your contacts within Dynamics AX show up with their names showing up as first and then last name.

To manually change the way that the contacts name show up, open up the record and then change the Name Sequence to LastCommaFirst.

Note: These formats are completely user configurable, so if you look into the details, then just drill into the details and you will see all of the formats, and also be able to add your own Name Sequences.

Now when you return to the list, the records name will be displayed with the last name first.

After a little maintenance, all of the contacts now show up the same way.

Rather than manually changing all of the records, you can set Dynamics AX up with a default Name Sequence so that all of your contacts show up wit their names the way that you like it. To do this, click on the Global Address Book Parameters menu item within the Global Address Book folder of the Setup group within the Organization Administration area page.

From within the General tab of the Global Address Book Parameters you can set the Name Sequence default.

Track Relationships Between Parties Through The Global Address Book

In addition to needing to track all of the common information within Dynamics AX like the Customers and Vendors, there is a lot of relationship information that you may want to record as well. You may want to track relationships between companies such as lenders, subsidiaries etc., between people such as recruiters, family members etc. or even between companies and people like board members, founders etc. The good news is that through the Global Address Book you can do just that.

Now we finally have a way to model the six degrees of Kevin Bacon.

How to do it...

Click on the Relationship Types menu item within the Global Address Book folder of the Setup group within the Organization Administration area page.

When the Relationship Types maintenance form is displayed you will see all of the different relationships that you can track by default within Dynamics AX.

You can also filter the types just to the ones that relate to a particular Party Type.

To create a relationship between the entities click on the Global Address Book menu within the Common group of the Home area page.

When the Global Address Book list page is displayed, open up the Party record that you want to create a relationship against and the jump to the Relationship tab.

To add a new Relationship click on the Add button within the tabs menu bar.

Then select the type of Relationship from the ID dropdown list.

Then select the A and B parties that you want to relate with each other.

Repeat the process until you have defined all of the relationships and then click the Close button.

Track Social Media Information Against Contacts

The contact management feature within Dynamics AX allows you to track an unlimited number of phone numbers, email addresses, and websites against a contact. But these are just the direct contact types. We live in the age of Social Media, and there are so many other different sources of information that we want to track against our contacts. Don't' despair, with a small tweak to the configuration within Dynamics AX, you can add additional contact media types and start tracking all this information.

Now you will be able to get the full scoop on you customers and contacts.

How to do it...

By default, Dynamics AX lets you track the common information against contacts like phone numbers, email addresses, web sites, and telex (who the heck even uses that).

To add more types to Dynamics AX, open up AOT, expand the Data Dictionary group, and then expand the Base Enums group.

Within the Base Enums, find the LogisticsElectronicAddressMethodTypes enumeration and expand it.

You will see all of the standard types are listed there.

Now right-mouse-click on the LogisticsElectronicAddressMethodTypes enumeration, and select the New Element menu item.

When the new element is created, change the Name and Label to be your new method type – in this case Twitter.

If you want to be an overachiever, then you can add a few more contact method types through AOT.

To test this, save your model and then restart Dynamics AX.

Now when you look at the types that are available for you within the Contact Information you will see that you have the option for all for the different social media types.

Now you can track everything properly.

How cool is that?

Schedule Multiple Discussions At Once Through The Mass Creation Option

Discussions are a polite term for being called into a meeting with HR, but the creation of them does not have to be a painful affair – at least for the HR department. There is a mass creation feature that allows you to create a block of discussion appointments for a group of employees that makes this process a breeze.

Being called into the principal's office has never been so automated.

How to do it...

Click on the Discussions menu item within the Performance folder of the Periodic group within the Human Resources area page.

When the Discussions maintenance form is displayed, click on the Mass Creation button in the menu bar.

When the Mass Create Discussions dialog box is displayed, enter in all of the discussion information and the date of the planned discussion.

If you want to refine the workers that are included in the discussion group, then you can click on the Select button and refine the selection criteria.

When you have set up your discussion template, just click on the OK button.

You will get an Infolog notification of all the discussions that have been created.

And when you return to the Discussions maintenance form you will see that everything has been scheduled for you.

Create Appointments In Outlook Directly From The Discussions

The only thing worse that having a "Discussion" with Human Resources is to miss a "Discussion", and have another "Discussion" created to discuss your poor time planning. To solve this, you may want to think about creating sending out meeting reminders when Discussions are created, which is just the click on the button within Dynamics AX.

Even if the discussion isn't pleasant, then at least the creation of one isn't.

How to do it...

Before you start, make sure that you have an e-mail address associated with your employees...

Click on the Discussions menu item within the Performance folder of the Periodic group within the Human Resources area page.

When the Discussions maintenance form is displayed, select the Discussion that you want to send out the appointment for and then click on the Copy To Microsoft Outlook button on the menu bar.

This will create an Outlook appointment for you with the date and time from the Discussion record, and also pre-populate it with the workers email address in the To box.

All you really need to do is click the Send button and the worker will have it on their calendar.

If you look at Outlook you will now see the appointment has been added to your calendar as well.

This is too organized.

Tally Packaging Quantities On Order Lines

If you are putting your products into boxes before you ship them out, or if you are worried about the cube space that the order lines will take up when being shipped then you might want to get Dynamics AX to calculate them on the fly as you enter in the order lines. The package calculation allows you to define how many items of a product goes into a standard package, and then it will tell you how many of those packages will be used on the order. For example, if you can fit 4 items in a box and the customer orders 6 then it will tell you that you need 2 boxes.

Now you can optimize you packing regardless of the product.

How to do it...

Click on the Packing Units menu item within the Packing Material folder of the Setup group within the Inventory Management area page.

Then the Packaging Units maintenance form is displayed, click on the New button in the menu bar to add a new packaging record.

Now just add an Item Relation for the product that you want to track the packaging quantity for, and enter the Packaging Unit and Packaging Unit Factor within the General tab.

When you are done configuring the packaging quantities, click on the Close button to exit from the form.

Now when you look at your Sales Order Lines, if you open up the Line Details tab, and then look within the Packing sub-tab, you will see that the Packing Material group shows the number of packages that you will need to the quantity.

To make this even better, right-mouse-click on the order line and select the Personalize option.

Then find the Packing Unit and Packing Unit Quantity fields and add them to the order lines table.

Now as you build up the order, the packing units will show up alongside the order quantities.

Isn't that so useful?

Generate Product Bar Code Labels Through Retail

The Retail area of Dynamics AX has a boat load of goodies embedded within it. One example of this is the capability to configure bar code labels for products that you can print at use for scanning and product identification. But just because it is configured through the Retail area it doesn't mean that you have to be a retail style company in order to take advantage of it. All you need to do is get over the stigma of the Retail label and set it up.

I know it feels naughty to use the Retail area, but it feels so good to do it...

How to do it...

First we need to do a little bit of setup to configure the bar codes themselves. And the first step is to configure the bar code Mask Characters.

To do this, click on the Mask Characters menu item within the Bar Codes and Labels folder of the Setup group within the Retail area page.

When the Bar Code Mask Characters maintenance form is displayed, click on the New button on the menu bar to add a new record.

For each different type of field that we are including in the bar code, we need to create a mask. For this example, select the Product option from the Type dropdown list.

Then set the Character to P.

Finally, add a Description and then click on the Close button to exit from the form.

Now we need to configure a mask to use on the bar codes. To do this, click on the Bar Code Mask Setup menu item within the Bar Codes and Labels folder of the Setup group within the Retail area page.

When the Bar Code Mask Setup maintenance form is displayed, click on the New button in the menu bar to create a new record.

Set the Mask ID, and Description, and then select the Product option from the Type dropdown list.

Then select the Bar Code Standard that you want to use to generate the bar code with.

And add a Prefix to the bar code record – I just used X for mine.

Then click on the Add button within the menu bar for the Bar Code Mask Segment to create a new segment within the bar code.

Set the Type to be Product and then set the Length of the bar code.

Now you will notice that the Mask field has been populated for you, and you can click on the Close button to exit from the form.

Now click on the Bar Code Setup menu item within the Bar Codes and Labels folder of the Setup group within the Retail area page.

When the Bar Codes maintenance form is displayed, click on the New button in the menu bar to create a new record.

Assign your new record a Bar Code Setup code, and also a Description.

Then select the same Bar Code Type as you configured in the previous step.

From the Mask ID dropdown, select the Mask that you just configured as well.

Set the Size field to be the font size that you want to use for the bar code.

And then set the Minimum and Maximum Length for the bar code.

When you have done that, just click on the Close button to exit from the form.

Nearly done with the setup. We just have to configure the label report. Do this by clicking on the Product Label Reports menu item within the Bar Codes and Labels folder of the Setup group within the Retail area page.

When the Product Label Report Setup maintenance form is displayed, click on the New button in the menu bar to create a new record.

Then select the label form that is delivered with Dynamics AX for the Item.

When you have done that, click on the Close button to exit from the form.

Now we can configure the bar codes for the products. To do this, open up the Released Products maintenance form, and click on the Bar Codes menu item within the Maintenance group of the Manage Inventory ribbon bar.

When the Item Bar Codes maintenance form is displayed it will automatically have a line shown in edit mode. You can create the Bar Code record by hand if you like, although a better way is to get Dynamics AX to do it. So click on the Delete button in the menu bar to remove the automatically created line.

Then click on the Create/Update Bar Codes menu item within the Functions dropdown menu.

When the Create Bar Codes dialog box is displayed, select the Bar Code Setup that you just configured from the dropdown list.

Then click on the OK button.

When the Create Bar Codes confirmation dialog box is displayed, click on the Yes button.

When you return to the Item Bar Codes maintenance form you will now have a bar code record.

Check the Scanning and Print check boxes, and then click the Close button to exit from the form.

Nearly there. All that is left now is to click on the Product Label button within the Setup group of the Retail ribbon bar.

When the Product Label Report Setup maintenance form is displayed, click on the New button within the menu bar to create a new record.

Select the Report Name from the dropdown list for the product label.

Then select a Distribution Group.

And finally select a Distribution Subgroup.

Now that you have the label configured, click on the Close button to exit from the form.

Now we can print our labels. To do that, click on the Print Specific Product Label button within the Functions group of the Retail ribbon bar.

When the Create Specific Product Label select the Report Name from the dropdown list, and then click on the OK button.

Now that's a pretty label.

Quickly Update Prices For Released Products

Updating prices through the standard Pricing Journals maintenance form can sometimes get a little unwieldy, especially when you just need to update one or two products. Fortunately if you want, you can update your prices directly from within the Released Products maintenance form, and with just a matter of clicks you will have a new and updated price list.

Now you can wheel and deal like a space cargo trader.

How to do it...

Open up the Released Products list page, select the product that you want to change the price for and then click on the View Trade Agreements button within the Trade Agreements group of the Sell ribbon bar.

When the View Trade Agreements inquiry is displayed you will see all of the current pricing for the product.

Select all of the lines that you want to update, and then click on the Edit Selected Lines button in the menu bar.

When the Select The Journal Name dialog box is displayed the Journal Name should already be populated, and all you need to do is click on the OK button.

Dynamics AX will open up the Journal Lines Price/Discount Agreement maintenance form with all of the old prices copied over into the journal.

Now you can just update the prices that you want to adjust, and when you are done, just click on the Post button in the menu bar.

When the Price/Discount Journal Posting dialog box is displayed, just click on the OK button.

When you return to the View Trade Agreements inquiry is displayed, you will see that the prices have now been updated based on your price journal.

How easy is that!

Mark Deleted Sales Orders As Voided To Track Lost Sales

Every sales order is special, even the deleted ones because they allow you to track you lost sales. If you don't want all of the deleted orders to disappear from Dynamics AX, then you can turn on the Voided Order Tracking and it will save all of the deleted order details for you for posterity.

Now your deleted sales orders will be gone, but not forgotten.

How to do it...

To turn on the voided order tracking click on the Accounts Receivable Parameters menu item within the Setup group of the Accounts Receivable area page.

Then check the Mark Order As Voided checkbox within the Setup group of the Sales tab in the General section.

Now go to any order that you don't need and click the Delete button within the Maintain group of the Sales Order ribbon bar.

And click the Yes button on the Confirm Deletion dialog box.

Now there is no trace of the order... or is there?

To see your deleted orders and lines, click on the Voided Sales Orders menu item within the History folder of the Inquiries group of the Sales And Marketing area page.

You will see the order that you just deleted is tracked here.

If you click on the Show button in the menu bar then you will see all of the history of the sales order that you voided as well.

Maybe you should bring some flowers next time...

Block Users From Using Particular Journal Names By Making Them Private

If the General Ledger is the heart and soul of Dynamics AX, and then the Journals are the DNA that builds up all of the information about the company. So it makes sense that you would want to make sure that people aren't just making postings willy nilly within the system. Some of the postings are automatic, some will be controlled through approval processes, but for the special journals that the finance department use, you may want to secure them down by making them private so that only certain people are able to see them.

The finance group is not a secret group, but that doesn't mean that it's not a group with secrets.

How to do it...

First you need to set up a user group that contains all of the users that you want to allow to use the journal. To do that, click on the User Groups menu item within the Users folder of the Common group of the System Administration area page.

When the User Group maintenance form is displayed, create a new record by pressing CTRL+N - there is no New button in the menu bar of this form, so you have to do this a little old school.

Then assign your User Group a Group name, and a description.

Then click on the Users tab, select the users that you want to include in the group, and then click on the < button.

After you have selected all of the users then you can click on the Close button to exit from the form.

Now we need to lock down the Journal by associating the User Group to it. To do this, click on the Journal Names menu item within the Journals folder of the Setup group within the General Ledger area page.

When the Journal Names maintenance form is displayed, select the Journal that you want to make private, and select the User Group that you just configured from the list within the Private For User Group drop down list within the Blocking section of the General tab.

After you have done that you are set, and you can click on the Close button to exit from the form.

Now, if you are not part of the cool kids that have access to the Journal you will not see it.

But for the lucky ones, it will show up on their list of available Journal Names.

Use Workflows To Process AP Invoices Through Unattached Documents

The Document Attachment feature within Dynamics AX is great, because you can attach files to any record in the system. But sometimes you have document attachments that do not have records that they can be attached to yet, and may have to create records and then attach them after the fact. In these cases you can take advantage of the unattached document feature and even add workflow processes around the document to make sure that it gets processed by the right people.

It's like matchmaking, except for files.

How to do it...

Start off by clicking on the Unattached Documents link within the Document Management folder of the Common group of the Home area page.

Select the document that you want to process and submit it to the Document Management workflow process.

Note: In this case we are linking the Unattached Document record to a scanned image that we have loaded into SharePoint.

Through the workflow process the AP clerk will be notified that they have a document that they need to process.

By following the Unattached Document link they are able to view the scanned image directly from within SharePoint.

- 159 –

The next step is to create the AP Invoice record based off the scanned image.

To attach the Unattached Document to the invoice for reference, click on the Attachments button within the Attachments group of the Vendor Invoices ribbon bar.

Then click on the New button in the menu bar and select the type of document that you want to associate the scanned invoice to.

In our case we will use the AP Invoice document type.

To search for the Unattached Document and link it to the attachment record, click on the Functions menu and click on the Select A Document File menu item.

This will give you a list of all the Unattached Documents. Just select the record for the scanned invoice, click on the Select button, and then click the Close button.

This will add a link to the document within SharePoint and you can even click on the Open button in the menu bar to view the record within SharePoint.

All that is left to do now is to return back to the work item list and complete the document management workflow.

Enable Change Management On Purchase Orders To Track Changes

If you want to track your Purchase Orders a little more closely, then you may want to turn on the Change Management feature within the Procurement & Sourcing module of Dynamics AX. This gives you the added ability to have workflow approvals on your Purchase Orders, but will also give you the ability to view the old versions of the Purchase Orders and see the differences between the versions.

Now you won't have to play "Spot The Difference" when trying to work out what was updated on the Purchase Order.

How to do it...

Normally if you create a Purchase Order within Dynamics AX you can immediately print out the Confirmation and then it is available for receiving.

If you look at the Approval Status on the record created, then they will normally have the Approved status as soon as they have been entered into the system.

To add more control to the Purchase Order generation process you can turn on the Change Control feature. To do this click on the Procurement and Sourcing Parameters menu item within the Setup group of the Procurement and Sourcing area page.

When the Procurement and Sourcing Parameters maintenance form is displayed, check the Activate Change Management flag within the Change Management For Purchase Orders group in the General page.

Purchase Orders that are tracked through Change Management are approved through the workflow engine within Dynamics AX. So there is one last step in the process and that is to create a new workflow that will allow you to approve the Purchase Orders when they are submitted.

Now create a new Purchase Order.

You will now notice that the Purchase Order has been set to a Draft approval status, and there is a submission option to send it to workflow for approval.

Also there is no option available to allow the user to confirm the Purchase Order. When you want to send the Purchase Order through the approval process, click on the Submit button.

This will change the status of the purchase order to In Review and then allow you to approve the PO.

Once the Purchase Order is approved you will be able to send out the Purchase Order confirmation.

Also, if you look at the Purchase Order ribbon bar, you will notice that the Edit option within the Maintain group is disabled, but the Request Change option is now enabled. To make an update to the Purchase Order, click on the Request Change button.

This will revert the Purchase Order back to a Draft approval status and the approval process needs to be completed before it is available to be sent out to the vendor again as a confirmation.

As a bonus, if you switch to the Manage ribbon bar, then the buttons within the History group of the ribbon bar will be enabled. If you want to see what the changes were over time, then click on the View Purchase Order History button.

When the Purchase Order Versions inquiry form is displayed, then you will see all of the different version of the Purchase Order.

To see the changes made, click on the Compare button within the menu bar.

This will show you all of the changes between the two Purchase Orders.

How cool is that!

Use Auto-Numbering Unless You Don't Feel Like It

If you have implemented some sort if intelligence within your numbering or naming schemes within Dynamics AX, then having it automatically assign a sequential number through auto-numbering completely messes up all of your hard work, but having your numbering as just a manual process also has it's disadvantages because you need to find the right slot to fit your number into as well. Dynamics AX has an option to allow you to override the automatic numbering that gets assigned though allowing you to accept the number it suggests, or change it up or down based on your preferences. This gives you the best of both worlds when it comes to numbering.

Who said you can't have your cake and eat it too.

How to do it...

In my system I have a simple scheme for numbering my products i.e. 1XXXXX for Raw Ingredients, 3XXXXX for Finished Goods, 4XXXXX for Packaging Supplies and 9XXXXX for Configured Products. Most of the time I will be adding new finished goods, so I want my numbering sequence to default in within the 3XXXXX series.

To do this, click on the Product Information Management Parameters menu item within the Setup group of the Product Information Management area page.

When the Product Information Management Parameters form is displayed, select the Number Sequence page, and then right-mouse-click on the Product Number number sequence and select View Details from the pop-up menu.

When the Number Sequence maintenance form is displayed, click on the Edit button within the Maintain group of the Number Sequence ribbon bar.

For this number sequence I have it set to manual so that I can enter in any number. To make this a semi-automated numbering sequence, uncheck the Manual flag within the General tab group.

Then set the Next number to the next number in the sequence that you want to use.

Also, check the To A Lower Number and To A Higher Number flags within the Allow User Changes group of the General tab group. This will allow the users to change the number even when it is auto-assigned.

Once you are done, you can click the Close button and exit out of the form.

Now when I create a new record, Dynamics AX will suggest the next product number in the sequence that I normally add products within.

But, if I want to change it then there is nothing stopping me from adding a higher or lower number.

Split Your Number Sequences To Make Them Look Intelligent

The Number Sequences within Dynamics AX are great because they allow you to add a lot of intelligence to your document and transaction numbering. You can add constants to them so that you can quickly see where they came from and sort though them. But it doesn't stop there. If you have incorporated some logic into how you are actually numbering the records, then you can split the number up itself so that even though it's still continuous, there may be segment separators that highlight that certain numbers are significant.

Now you just need to train the users on what the numbers mean...

How to do it...

In my system I have a simple scheme for numbering my products i.e. 1XXXXX for Raw Ingredients, 3XXXXX for Finished Goods, 4XXXXX for Packaging Supplies and 9XXXXX for Configured Products. So I would really like to highlight this by separating out the first number when I create the products so that it has the format X-XXXXX.

To do this, click on the Product Information Management Parameters menu item within the Setup group of the Product Information Management area page.

When the Product Information Management Parameters form is displayed, select the Number Sequence page, and then right-mouse-click on the Product Number number sequence and select View Details from the pop-up menu.

When the Number Sequence maintenance form is displayed, click on the Edit button within the Maintain group of the Number Sequence ribbon bar.

Our original Number Sequence in this example is 6 digits long, and is one continuous number string. Click on the Add button within the menu bar of the Segments tab group.

When the new segment record is created, change the Segment to Constant.

Then set the Value to -.

Repeat the process and add another Alphanumeric Segment and set the Value to #####.

So that there are still only 6 places in the total number of Alphanumeric placeholders, set the first Alphanumeric segment mask to #.

Note: Since the mask has 6 # placeholders then the numbers that are allocated to the sequence will remain the same even though there are 7 characters in the full product number record.

Now when I go out and create a new Product In Dynamics AX, it will format the number with my intelligent number separator after the first character.

Now if only I had done this from the start, then all of the products would have looked intelligent.

Use Pricing Models Within Configured Products To Calculate Prices Without A BOM

The Product Configurator within Dynamics AX is very cool and is a great way to capture options during the sales and quoting process. You don't have to go whole hog with it though and have it build BOM's and Routes in order to have it help you during the sales cycle in quoting prices though. The Product Configurator has a built in Price Modeler feature that allows you to design a price build up based on your configuration attributes, and then calculate prices dynamically as you are placing your orders.

You will now be able to rest easy that all of the costs have been taken into account when you price out jobs.

How to do it...

Start off by designing your configured product with all the options that you want to capture and then click on the Price Models button within the Setup group of the Model ribbon bar.

When the Price Models maintenance form is displayed, add a new record, and then click on the Edit button in the menu bar.

This will open up the Price Model designer. Click on the Add button within the Expression Rules tab to add a new price component.

Give your Expression a Name, and then click on the down-arrow on the Condition field to open up the condition editor.

When the Expression Editor is displayed, you can build your expression rule just by pointing and clicking through the columns. When you are done, just click on the OK button.

Then add a component price to the Expression field.

Note: You can also build an expression here as well like you did with the Condition field and use a formula to calculate the price.

Continue adding additional Expression Rules to the pricing model for all the components that affect the price.

When you are done, just click on the Test button to see it in action.

When the Test form is displayed, you will notice that there is a Price being calculated on the right in the fact boxes.

If you change the options within the product configuration, then the price changes as well.

If you want to see a breakdown of the prices in Excel, then click on the View Price Breakdown button.

Dynamics AX will build you an Excel workbook with a summary of the prices.

How cool is that!

To use this within your Sales Orders, there is a little bit more setup required. Start off by clicking on the Price Model Criteria button within the Set Up group of the Model ribbon bar.

When the Price Model Criteria maintenance form is displayed, add a record, link it to the Price Model that you just created and also select the Sales Order type from the Order Type field.

When you are done then click on the Close button.

Also, you need to make sure that your product configuration is configured to use the pricing model. To do this, click on the Versions button within the Product Model Definition group of the Model area page.

When the Versions maintenance form is displayed, make sure that the Pricing Method for the record is Attribute Based.

To see this in action, add a new Sales Order add a line for your configured product, and then configure it by clicking on the Configure Line option within the Product And Supply line menu item.

As you configure the line on the sales order, you will see the price is being updated based on the choices.

Also, when you return to the Sales Order the price that was calculated through the configuration is updated and applied to the order line.

Now that is super cool.

Control Price Adjustments On Sales Orders

You probably spend a lot of time trying to set up your pricing within Dynamics AX so that it is just right, and then the salespeople come along and just change it willey nilley as they are taking the sales orders. If a price change feels like a needle piercing your heart then don't worry, you can turn off the ability for the users to be able to update the price that you have set up, or at the very least, turn on reason codes so that when a price is changed, the user has to say why they made the change.

At least now when the users break your heart and ignore the suggested pricing, you will know why and receive a little closure.

How to do it...

Open up your Released Product that you want to control the price updates on and within the Price Adjust field group of the Sell fast tab, notice that there is a new field called Allow Price Adjust.

To lock the price then uncheck this box.

When you place an order for that product, there will be no way that the user is able to change the default price.

If you want to allow the users to change the price, then check the Allow Price Adjust flag.

Now when you change the price on the order a Change Reason dialog box will be displayed.

You will be required to select a reason from the reason codes that have been assigned to price changes.

After selecting the reason code, just click the OK button.

Now the price has been updated, and also an icon will show up on the order line that indicates that the price has been adjusted.

Also, the line details will be highlighted to give a visual cue that the price has been adjusted.

Tip: If you want to change the default color for the price change highlighter, then click on the Call Center Parameters within the Setup group of the Call Center area page.

Within the Display page of the Properties you will find a color field called Price Override Line that you can change to any other color you like for the line highlighting.

Create Filtered Alerts To Sniff Out The Data You Really Want

Alerts are a great feature within Dynamics AX because they allow you to watch any information that you are interested in and then get alerts when the information is changed or updated. This is great for when you need status updates but are too busy (or lazy) to go into the list pages and look for yourself. But alerts are a double edged sword. If you are not careful you can end up spamming yourself. Having too much information being sent to you is just as bad as none at all. Luckily you can fine tune your alerts and notifications down from the shotgun approach to just the information that you are interested in.

It's like having your very own truffle sniffing pig, except it's not a pig and it sniffs out data, so really nothing like a truffle sniffing pig...

How to do it...

Start off by finding the data that you want to get alerted on. In this case we want to watch the status of our Sales Orders so we will watch the Status field. Then right-mouse-click on the field and select the Create Alert Rule menu item.

When the Create Alert Rule dialog box is displayed, change the Event to Is Set To so that we can track when the orders are placed in a certain status.

Then select the Status that you want to be notified on from the second dropdown list. In this case we only want to know when the orders are invoiced.

Then change the Subject and Message so that the alert is a little more informational.

If you expand out the Alert Who group then you will be able to choose who is notified.

Also if you expand out the Other Alerts group then you can choose if you want to receive a Pop-Up, and/or an Email.

To make this even more useful we can restrict the records further to just the ones that we are interested in. In order to do this, click on the Select button within the Alert Me For group.

This will open up the default selection for this alert. To add another condition to this selection, click on the Add button.

This will create a new line within the Range tab. You can then select the Field that you want to filter this alert on. In this case we will filter further on the Sales Responsible field so that we only get alerted on the orders that we are connected with.

Then from the Criteria field we can select the user that we want to filter the selection on.

You can continue refining the search, and when you are done, click on the OK button to save the selection.

Now that you have created the alert, just click on the OK button to exit form.

To see this in action, we will start off with our records that we want to watch.

Just to be sure with this example we will make sure that the user is associated with the order before we continue on.

All that we need to do is invoice the sales order.

Behind the scenes Dynamics AX will send the user a notification that the order has been invoiced.

If you drill into the notification details then the subject and message will be copied from the alert to the notification as well.

How cool is that.

Declutter Customer Lists By Securing Them Through Address Books

Sometimes giving everyone access to every contact within the global address book is not necessary. Maybe you want to show people only contacts within their region, or legal entity, maybe you want to hide away inactive contacts from the default lists, or maybe you are just paranoid and don't want to give people access to all the contacts in the system. Regardless of the reason, you can do this easily with a click of the switch within Dynamics AX through the Address Book Security feature.

Now you can keep your special client list away from prying eyes.

How to do it...

Just to show that there is nothing up my sleeves, this is the user before making this change. They have access to all of the contacts by default.

The first step to lock down the contact information is to set up some address books that we can use to classify them. To do this click on the Address Books menu item within the Global Address Book folder of the Setup group within the Organization Administration area page.

If when the Address Books maintenance form is displayed you don't have any records, just click on the New button in the ribbon bar to create new record.

Now that we have address books configured we can start assigning them to the Customer records. To do this, open up your Customers detail page, and within the General fast tab, click on the Address Books field and select all of the address books that you want to assign to the customer record.

Repeat this for all the customers and then close out of the form.

Note: Any record that does not have an address book record will be treated as globally available.

Dynamics AX restricts access to the Address Books by Teams to make the administration easier. So we need to make sure that we have some Teams defined. To do this, click on the Teams menu item within the Organization folder of the Setup group within the Organization Administration area page.

When the Teams maintenance form is displayed, make sure that all of your employees are configured within a Team and then close out of the form.

Now we will enable the security around the contacts. To do this, click on the Global Address Book Parameters menu item within the Global Address Book folder of the Setup group within the Organization Administration area page.

When the Global Address Book Parameters maintenance form is displayed, select the Security Policy Options page.

To secure the address books, just click on the Secure By Address Book check box.

Note: When you save the change (CTRL+S) then Dynamics AX actually updates the database security so you may notice the log file trace pops up. After this is done, you can close the info panel.

Now that the security has been enabled, we need to specify who has access to the Address Books. To do this, click on the Assign Teams button.

When the Assign Teams To Address Books maintenance form is displayed, select the Address Book that you want to secure.

Then select all of the Teams that you want to give access to this address book from the Available Teams list and click the Add>> button.

This will add them to the Selected Teams panel.

Repeat the process for all of the other Address Books and when you are done, click on the Close button to exit from the form.

Now when our users look at the Customers, they only see the ones that they have been assigned.

Who said security is hard.

Set Default Parameter Values Into Posting Forms

There are usually a lot of different configuration choices that you can make choose from when you are performing updates and selections within the Dynamics AX forms. But you probably only use one option on a daily basis. Rather than going in and changing the selection parameters every time you open up the form, Dynamics AX allows you to set the default values and from then on you will always have the right parameters in your form.

This is definitely a case of set it and forget it.

How to do it...

On some of the posting forms, you will notice that there is a Default button to the right of the form. If you want to change the default parameters that are used in the form, just click on it.

When the Set Up Default Parameters dialog box is displayed you will see all of the default values that are used for the form.

All you need to do is change them to what you want to use from now on and then click the Close button.

Now when you come into the form, all of the defaults will be applied, and you can just continue on without hitting a road bump.

That is so useful.

OFFICE TRICKS

It's no secret that everyone uses Office to create documents and reports, and that's fine. But if you really want to use Office, then you should take advantage of all the integration that is built into it for Dynamics AX.

Don't just cut and paste your spreadsheets, link them to Dynamics AX. Don't just use Excel as a worksheet to help you with your updates, make it the way that you update Dynamics AX. Don't just copy data to Word documents, make them templates that are automatically updated. Don't just use Project for recording project information, make it a tool that updates Dynamics AX.

In this section we will uncover how you can use some of the integrated Office features to make you a Dynamics AX ninja.

Topics Covered

- Export to Excel when there is no Ribbon Bar

- Exporting Data To Your Client's Excel When Using Remote Desktop

- Add Additional Dynamics AX Fields To Worksheets After Exporting To Excel

- Use the Export to Excel To Create Your Own Refreshable Reports In Excel

- Create Reports Directly Off The Dynamics AX Cubes Through Excel

- Update Dynamics AX Records Through Excel Using The Excel Add-in

- Create Reports For Dynamics AX From Within Word

- Populate Boilerplate Document With Dynamics AX Data Using Word Templates

- Use Word Templates to Generate Standard Customer Correspondence

- Update Your Project Plans Using Microsoft Project

- Create Projects In Dynamics AX Directly From Microsoft Project

- Make the Dynamics AX Role Center Your Outlook Home Page

- Use Lync to Track People Down Directly From Dynamics AX

- Synchronize Dynamics AX With Microsoft Outlook

- Synchronize Your Contacts Between Dynamics AX And Outlook And Back Again

- Perform Field Lookups Directly From Excel

- Make Excel Exports Static By Disabling the Refresh Option

- Creating Document Attachment Templates Using Word

Export to Excel when there is no Ribbon Bar

Not all of the forms within Dynamics AX have the ribbon bar enabled with the Export to Excel icon handy for you to use when you want to gram a copy of the data, but that doesn't mean that there is no way to quickly get your data moved over to a linked worksheet.

All you need to do is select the Export to Microsoft Excel menu item from the Files menu, or for those of you that love shortcut keys, just press CTRL+T and Dynamics AX will create an Excel Workbook with all of the data from the form populated in it.

How to do it...

Select the Export to Microsoft Excel menu item from the Files menu.

Note: Your can also just press CTRL+T if you like using keyboard shortcuts.

Now all of the data in the current form will be exported to a new Excel workbook.

Exporting Data To Your Client's Excel When Using Remote Desktop

Just because you are using a remote desktop to access Dynamics AX, doesn't mean that you have to do everything there. One example of this is that you can choose to export data to your local version of Excel rather than to the version of Office that may be running on your remote desktop. All you need is to change one of the options within the Dynamics AX client.

This allows you to work with the exported data after you are disconnected from the remote desktop, it allows you to use any additional extensions that you may have installed on your local machine within Excel, and most importantly saves you the hassle of having to cut and paste the worksheet from the remote desktop over to your local machine.

How to do it...

From the Files menu select the Tools submenu, and then the Options menu item.

When the Options dialog box is displayed, scroll down to the Miscellaneous section, and change the Remote Desktop session export to option to Client Excel.

Now when you click the Export to Microsoft Excel it will send all of your data to the client version of Excel.

Note: Make sure that the user that you are using on the client desktop has the login information for Dynamics AX and also security to access the data, because the security policies that are in effect on the client are associated with that user login… This also ensures that people are not sidestepping the security policies by doing this.

Add Additional Dynamics AX Fields To Worksheets After Exporting To Excel

Exporting to Excel from Dynamics AX is probably one of the most used features for all of the do-it-yourselfers out there because once the data is in Excel you can create your own reports, dashboards, and analysis in a tool that we are all very familiar with.

But just because Dynamics AX exports the fields that are showing on the form does not mean that you have to settle for that data. Using the Dynamics AX Add-In for Excel, you can see all of the fields that are available within the table or query from Excel and add in new columns on the fly, making your Excel queries even more useful.

How to do it...

Start off by finding the query within Dynamics AX that you want to use, and then click on the Export to Excel button in the ribbon bar.

When the worksheet is created within Excel, click on the Fields button in the Design group of the Dynamics AX ribbon bar.

This will show you the field explorer panel, and you will be able to see all of the related fields that you can also add to the worksheet. Just drag the fields over to the worksheet to use them. In this case I just pulled over the Net amount field.

Now you can click on the Fields button again to return to Edit mode, and then click on the Refresh button within the Data group of the Dynamics AX ribbon bar, and you will now see all the fields, including the new ones that you added are updated in the worksheet.

Use the Export to Excel To Create Your Own Refreshable Reports In Excel

When you have the Dynamics AX Add-In for Excel installed, the Export to Excel function within Dynamics AX automatically links the data table that you exported back to the data within Dynamics AX. This means that you are able to refresh the data at any time, returning back the latest information without having to re-export from the client.

Once you have created the linked worksheet, you can build your own dashboards and reports from it within Excel and they will always be up to date.

How to do it...

Start off within the Dynamics AX form that you want to create a report from and click the Export To Excel button. If there is no button, just press CTRL+T.

This will open up Excel and transfer all of the data that was on the query within Dynamics AX over there, including any filters that you may have applied.

What makes this so useful is that if you click on the Fields button within the Design group of the Dynamics AX ribbon bar, you will see that the worksheet is linked back to Dynamics AX and you can add new fields, and also refresh the data at any time.

So, if we create a new PowerView dashboard based off the data...

And then update the data within Dynamics AX...

We can click on the Refresh button within the Data group of the Dynamics AX ribbon bar, and our data in the worksheet will be instantly updated.

And so will our dashboard.

All of this is done without writing a single line of code.

Create Reports Directly Off The Dynamics AX Cubes Through Excel

Excel is probably the number one reporting tool because it is on everyone's computer, and also because it is so easy to manipulate the data and create your own analysis, charts and tables. In the past though, the more technical users have had a slight advantage over the general users because they knew the secret table combinations that allowed them to piece data together directly from the database, giving them better insight and reports, whilst the less technical users had to resort to cutting and pasting data, or transcribing pieces of information from other reports into Excel which made their reports tedious to build and also prone to errors.

Those days are over though because Dynamics AX comes pre-delivered with a set of reporting cubes that have already simplified and summarized the data from you and you can connect to it directly from Excel. This makes reporting so much easier for everyone, and also makes sure that everyone has the same results when they create their reports.

How to do it...

If this is the first time that you have connected to the Dynamics AX Cubes, then you will need to create a data connection within Excel. You will only have to do this once, because Excel will remember the connection.

To do this, select the Data ribbon bar, and click on the From Other Sources button from within the Get External Data group. From the dropdown, select the From Analysis Services menu item.

When the Data Connection Wizard dialog box is displayed, type in the name of the server where your cubes are store on, and then click on the Next button.

The next page will ask you to select the cube that you want to connect to. If you uncheck the Connect to a specific cube or table option, then you will be able to re-use this connection over and over again and connect to any of the 18 different areas without creating a new connection.

All you need to do now is select the cube that you want to create a report off, and click the Next button.

Finally, give your connection a name (or leave it as the default name) and then click on the Finish button.

Excel will then ask you how you want to report off the data – a PivotTable Report will work fine for this example – and then click the OK button.

This will open up a worksheet with the blank PivotTable on the left, and all of the cube dimensions and measures on the right. All of the data has been distilled down into a set of groups and names that everyone should be able to understand.

To create a report you just need to select the items that you want and add them to the PivotTable.

Update Dynamics AX Records Through Excel Using The Excel Add-in

The Excel Add-In does more than just download data to Excel, you can also use it to publish data back to Dynamics AX, making it a great tool for performing mass imports of records, and also for tweaking your data after you have it within Dynamics AX.

This is a much better option than ODBC connections, which has been the usual method that people use to connect and update data because all of the updates are performed through Dynamics AX, so if there are rules, or security considerations that have been put in place, then the update will honor them.

How to do it...

Open up Excel, and select the Add Tables menu item from Add Data menu button within the Design group of the Dynamics AX ribbon bar.

This will open up the Select Tables dialog box listing all of the tables within Dynamics AX.

You can filter the tables by tying in all or part of the table name within the Filter field.

To add the table to the worksheet, just select it and then click on the > button to move it to the Selected Tables panel. When you have selected all the tables that you want to update, just click on the OK button to exit the form.

When you are returned to Excel, a worksheet for each of the tables would have been created for you with all of the key fields, and also the Field Explorer will be displayed on the left showing all of the available fields associated with the table.

You can add additional fields to the worksheet just by dragging them from the Field Explorer over to the worksheet table.

When you have finished adding the additional fields to the worksheet, click on the Fields button within the Design group of the Dynamics AX ribbon bar to return to edit mode.

Then to retrieve all of the data from Dynamics AX, click on the Refresh button within the Data group of the Dynamics AX ribbon bar.

Now your worksheet will be populated with all of the data from Dynamics AX.

To update Dynamics AX, all you need to do is update the rows within Excel, and then click on the Publish All menu item from the Publish menu button within the Update group of the Dynamics AX ribbon bar.

This will create an additional tab that shows the status of the update and also showing how many records have been updated.

Returning to Dynamics AX we will see that all of the data has now been updated.

How simple is that!

Create Reports For Dynamics AX From Within Word

The Office Add-Ins for Dynamics AX are great, and most people are familiar with the Excel Add-In, but don't forget about the Word Add-In. This allows you to create documents that are use data from Dynamics AX, almost like a mail merge, giving you the ability to create custom reports without having to get your IT department involved.

This allows you to create summary documents, or internal reports that you are able to format just like you would any other Word document, and also reuse over and aver again if you need to.

How to do it...

Open Word, and you should be able to see the Dynamics AX ribbon bar that is added when the Dynamics AX Add-In's for Office were installes.

To start creating your document, click on the Add Data button within the Design group.

This will open up a dialog box that shows you all of the published data sources that you can use within Word. In this case we will select the Sales orders query.

A new Dynamics AX panel will show up on the left of the document with all of the available fields that you can add to the report.

If you create a table in the document, then you will be able to drag the fields over to create a grid template.

Note: Just create a table that is 2 rows high, and drag the field into the second row, allowing the Add-In to automatically add a heading in the first row.

After you have done that, save the report.

Now, return to the Dynamics AX ribbon bar, and click on the Merge button within the Data group.

This will create a new Word document for you based off the template with all the data being populated from Dynamics AX.

Populate Boilerplate Document With Dynamics AX Data Using Word Templates

The document management function that allows you to create attachments that are based off a Word template. What makes this a super useful feature is that you can populate the document on the fly with data from the record that you are creating the attachment for.

Everyone has templates that they have squirreled away on their computer that they continually use for boilerplate responses. This takes it to the next level by creating all of these document for you based of the boilerplate documents... and they are not hidden on one persons computer any more.

How to do it...

Start off by creating your template document.

To add a placeholder for the data within Dynamics AX, move the cursor to the location that you want to data to go, and then click on the Links menu button within the Comments group of the Insert ribbon bar, and select the Bookmark menu item.

When the Bookmark maintenance dialog is displayed, enter in the name for the placeholder and then click the Add button.

When you are finished, just close the form.

After you have finished adding in all of the bookmarks, save the file as a .dot file type.

Now click on the Document Types menu item within the Document Management folder of the Setup group within the Organization Administration area page.

Click on the New button within the menu bar to create a new record, give your document type a Type and Name, and then change the Class to Create a Microsoft Word document by using a Template.

This will enable the Options button within the menu bar that you should now click on.

When the Setup maintenance form is displayed, add a new record (CTRL+N) and select the main table that you want to associate the data from (in this case the CustTable table) and then point the Template file to your Word Template.

Change to the Fields tab, and add a new record for each of your bookmarks that you added to the template document. Select the Data field that you want to embed in the template and type in the Bookmark that you want to put the field value into.

When you have finished with all of the bookmarks, then just click on the OK field to exit the form.

Now when you attach document to the document types where the master table matches the linked table in the new document type that you created

This will automatically create your personalized version of the document for you.

How cool is that

Use Word Templates to Generate Standard Customer Correspondence

You probably have already used the Dynamics AX add-in within Excel to access data, but don't forget that you can also do something similar within Word as well in order to create templates that will merge in data directly from Dynamics AX with the push of a button. But it doesn't stop there, you can then save the Word templates back to a template library and Dynamics AX will make it available to everyone through the client itself.

This is a great way to create lightweight reports or commonly used templates for correspondence that you have instant access to.

How to do it...

Before you start, you need to make sure that you have a query that Word is able to use as a data source. Also, this query needs to be linked in some way to the master tables that are used in the main data forms, i.e. the CustTable.

If you have not already got queries defined, then you can do this by clicking on the Document Data Sources in the Document Management folder of the Setup group of the Organization Administration area page.

When the Document Data Sources maintenance form is displayed, click on the New button in the menu bar, and add a new record that has a Document Source Type of Query Reference and a Data Source Name of CustTable

When you have done this, just click on the Close button to exit the form.

To create a template in Word, all you need to do is select the Dynamics AX ribbon bar and click on the Add Data button within the Design group.

When the Add Data dialog box is displayed, you can select the CustTable data source and then click the OK button.

This will open up a field explorer on the left which you can then just drag and drop any field from into the Word document in order to create field placeholders.

Additionally, if you create a table within the word document then you can create a repeating element.

Once you have created the template you can save it and then click on the Merge button within the Data group of the Dynamics AX ribbon bar.

This will create a new document that is populated with the data from Dynamics AX.

The next step is to make this template available to the users within Dynamics AX itself. To do this, create a Document Library within SharePoint and save your new template there.

Once we have the document library, we just need to synchronize it with Dynamics AX by opening up the Document Types menu item within the Document Management folder of the Setup group of the Organization Administration area page.

If you don't already have one, create a new Document Type with a Class of Template Library. This will allow you to point to the SharePoint Site where you put your Word document, and then click the Synchronize button within the Document Templates tab.

This process should discover your document and then you can make it available by clicking on the If you don't already have one, create a new Document Type with a Class of Template Library. This will allow you to point to the SharePoint Site where you put your Word document, and then click the Active checkbox.

This will allow you to open up the master data form that is connected to your Word template (in this case the Customer maintenance form) and if you click on the Generate From Template button within the Attachments group of the Customer ribbon bar, you will see your document template is available to be selected.

Clicking on it will create a new Word document for you using the merge template that you created.

Also, it saves the document away as an attachment so that you can always reference back to it.

How cool is that.

Update Your Project Plans Using Microsoft Project

With the CU7 release of Dynamics AX, a new feature was added to the Projects area that allows you to link your projects with Microsoft Project so that you can update the work breakdown structures visually Microsoft Project, and then have all of the changes automatically update Dynamics AX.

Updating project plans will never be a chore again.

How to do it...

Select the project that you want to link and manage through Microsoft Project, and click on the Open in Microsoft Project button within the Activities group of the Plan ribbon bar.

This will open up Microsoft Project with all of your work breakdown structure from the Dynamics AX project configured as a Microsoft Project project plan.

You can update all of the project details directly within Microsoft project, and when you have finished and want to update Dynamics AX, just close Microsoft Project.

This will kick off an update that will save all of the changes back to Dynamics AX.

If you look at the project within Dynamics AX, you will now see an icon to the left of the project information that shows that it has been linked with Microsoft Project.

And if you look at the Work Breakdown Structure for the project, it will reflect the changes that you made within Microsoft Project.

Create Projects In Dynamics AX Directly From Microsoft Project

Every one knows that you can now edit your Dynamics AX projects directly in Microsoft Project, but the integration gets even cooler then that. If you have an existing project plan that you want to turn into a new project, then you can create it directly from Microsoft Project itself.

This is a super easy way to migrate all of your old projects over to Dynamics AX.

How to do it...

Just to prove that there was no project in the system before doing this, we can check the current projects.

Open up your project plan within Microsoft Project and select the Publish New Project menu item from the Publish button within the Update group of the Dynamics AX ribbon bar.

Dynamics AX will then remind you that the project plan is going to be copied over to the server. Just click the OK button.

When the Publish as a New Project dialog box is displayed, although you can change any of the defaults here, you will just need to give your project a Name and then click on the OK button to create your project in Dynamics AX.

Now when you return to the Projects list, you will see that there is a new project that has been created.

If you open up the project, then all of the core information for the project has already been populated for you.

And all of the Work Breakdown Structure has been loaded as well.

How easy is that!

Make the Dynamics AX Role Center Your Outlook Home Page

The Role Centers are web pages that you can run independently of the client, and are designed to give you a lightweight way to access most of the functions within Dynamics AX. Since they are just web pages then they can also be embedded in other applications that you may use all of the time, like Outlook, to give you another way to view the status of the organization.

This is a great way to let users that are not normally accessing Dynamics AX all of the time view the status of the organization, since they cannot avoid opening up Outlook.

How to do it...

Access the Enterprise Portal through a web browser. The usual website address is:

http://servername/sites/DynamicsAx/Enterprise%20Portal/

Note: When you open up the Enterprise Portal through the browser, you will get a little more information that you do when it is seen within the Dynamics AX client. You have a title bar along the top, and also a web menu bar on the left.

If you add the following two qualifiers to the end of the URL, then your Enterprise Portal will become a lot cleaner.

&runonclient=1&isdlg=1

Now open up Outlook, and right-mouse-click on your account header and select the Data File Properties menu item.

When the Data File Properties dialog box is displayed, click on the Home Page tab, and past the role center URL into the Address field. The format will look something like this:

http://servername/sites/DynamicsAx/Enterprise%20Portal/RoleCenterCFO.aspx?&runonclient=1&isdlg=1

Now when you return to Outlook, you will see the Role Center as the Outlook home page.

Use Lync to Track People Down Directly From Dynamics AX

Lync is a great way to communicate with all of the people that you work with since you can easily see if people are available, and then instantly start an instant message, voice call, or a video conferencing session. It is also fully integrated with Dynamics AX, allowing you to start Lync communications without even having to search for the person within Lync.

This is a great tool for the users because they can instantly connect with other people in the company, especially when you are researching a problem, or want to ask questions about something that was entered into Dynamics AX by someone else. All you have to do is click and call.

How to do it...

There is one setup step that is required in order to enable to Lync with the people within the organization, and that is to tell Dynamics AX what email address to use for the people when searching for them through Lync.

To do this you need to open up the Worker records, and make sure that their Lync email address is registered against the Contact Information.

You also need to check that the Instant message and Instant message sign-in flags are checked against the Lync email address.

Now when you see any of the users referenced within Dynamics AX, you will see the Lync presence bubble, and if you click on the bubble, you will be able to start Lync calls directly from there.

Synchronize Dynamics AX With Microsoft Outlook

Although we would like to be sitting in front of Dynamics AX all the time, it's usually just not the case because we're travelling, or just away from our desks. All that time, people may be setting up meetings for you, assigning critical tasks, or updating contact information that maybe you will need.

You don't have to miss a beat though because you can set up your Dynamics AX client so that it synchronizes with Microsoft Outlook, and then all of the tasks, appointments, and contacts that you use will travel with you on your laptop, tablet, and even your phone.

How to do it...

Before we start, there is one small piece of housekeeping that you need to perform before configuring the synchronization. Dynamics AX and Outlook pair themselves through the e-mail account that is associated with your client. So start off by selecting the Options menu item from the Tools submenu of the Files menu.

When the Options dialog box is displayed, check that the E-mail account is the same as the account that you use for Microsoft Outlook.

To set up the pairing between your Dynamics AX client and Outlook, select the Microsoft Outlook setup wizard option from the Setup group of the Home area page.

Step through the wizard until you get to the Microsoft Outlook synchronization page, and click on the Use current Microsoft Outlook profile button to link the profiles. If your e-mail addresses match then your name should show up in the Microsoft Office Outlook user identification field.

Next click on the Pick contact Microsoft Outlook folder button, and choose the folder in Outlook that you want to synchronize the contacts to.

Repeat this for the tasks, and also the appointments, and then set a number of days in the past and future that you want to synchronize.

Then you can continue through the wizard and exit the setup.

To synchronize Dynamics AX with Outlook, just click on the Synchronize menu item within the Microsoft Outlook synchronization folder of the Periodic group of the Home area page.

Select the elements that you want to synchronize, and then click the OK button to synchronize.

Now all of your appointments, tasks, and contacts will be over in Outlook.

Synchronize Your Contacts Between Dynamics AX And Outlook And Back Again

If you have linked Dynamics AX with your local version of Microsoft Outlook, then you have probably ran the synchronization that adds all of the appointments, tasks, and also the contacts to Outlook. But there is a more powerful option that allows you to synchronize not only from Dynamics AX and Outlook, but with Outlook back to Dynamics AX giving you an even more useful form of contact synchronization.

This is a great way to keep your contacts up to date, and also to populate Dynamics AX with all of your contact data without having to key in all of the people by hand, and also keep it up to date because it synchronizes both ways.

Remember, a contact does not become less useful if you share it with your friends.

How to do it...

Start of by adding contacts to Dynamics AX.

Then click on the Synchronize menu item within the Microsoft Outlook Synchronization folder of the Periodic group of the Home area page.

When the My Contacts maintenance form is displayed, to synchronize the contacts within Dynamics AX to Outlook, click on the Add contacts from Microsoft Dynamics menu item under the Add contacts menu item.

When the Select contacts from Microsoft Dynamics AX dialog box is displayed, all of the contacts that have not currently been synchronized with Outlook will be displayed. Check all of the contacts that you want to synchronize and then click on the Add to my contacts button.

When you return to My contacts all the contacts will now have an link back to Outlook.

If you open up Outlook then all of the contact information will be synchronized.

Next, add a contact within Outlook that doesn't exist within Dynamics AX.

One tip is to ensure that the Country/Region for the address is United States.

Return to the My Contacts maintenance form is displayed, and to synchronize the contacts within Outlook with Dynamics AX, click on the Add contacts from Microsoft Outlook menu item under the Add contacts menu item.

When the Select contacts from Microsoft Outlook dialog box is displayed, all of the contacts that have not currently been synchronized Outlook to Dynamics AX will be displayed.

Check all of the contacts that you want to synchronize and also add the Contact for which will be the company that you want to associate the contact with.

When you are finished, click on the Create button.

When you return to My contacts all the contacts from Outlook will now be added to the list of synchronized contacts.

For any of the contacts, where they originated within Outlook, you can update the records information – like the phone number, or the email address.

To update Dynamics AX, all you need to do is click on the Synchronize button within the menu bar of the My Contacts maintenance form.

When you look at the contact within Dynamics AX, the details will be changed.

How slick is that!

Perform Field Lookups Directly From Excel

The Dynamics AX Add-In for Excel is a great tool for downloading and updating data from Dynamics AX within a tool that everyone is familiar with. But not everyone is familiar with all of the valid values that are allowed for the fields. Don't worry though the Excel Add-In has a nifty lookup function that allows you to find out what valid values are allowed.

No more searching for field values by trial and error.

How to do it...

When accessing Dynamics AX data from Excel, select the filed that you want to look up on, and click on the Lookup button within the Data group on the Dynamics AX ribbon bar.

The Dynamics AX Add-In will then open up a dialog box with all of the valid values that you can enter into the field.

All you need to do is select the value, and then click on the OK button.

Make Excel Exports Static By Disabling the Refresh Option

The Export To Excel function within Dynamics AX is a powerful tool, because it gives you a live link back to the database, allows you to add additional fields, and also allows you to refresh the data. But for some people that is just too much power. For those users you can easily turn the Export To Excel from a power tool to a simple screen scrape utility just with a flick of a option flag.

I would never suggest that you do this as an April Fools prank...

How to do it...

Click on the Files menu, select the Tools submenu, and then click on the Options menu item.

When the Options maintenance form is displayed, select the General page, and change the Workbook Supports Refresh option within the Export to Microsoft Excel group of the Miscellaneous tab from When Possible to Never.

Now just go to any form that you would normally export data from, and click on the Export To Microsoft Excel button.

When Excel opens up with your data, you will notice that you are not able to refresh any of the data from within Excel, because this is now just a simple export rather than a live connection.

Creating Document Attachment Templates Using Word

In the perfect world, all documents and reports that are created out of Dynamics AX should be created within Reporting Services, sometimes don't have the time or the resources available to create the reports, so you end up resorting to using other tools like Word or Excel to create quick and dirty versions. I'm not judging you all, because you have to do what you have to do, but if you do use Office as a reporting tool, then there is a feature within Dynamics AX that allows you to save your Word documents as templates and then link data directly from the system into the document, and also automatically save the document that is created as a document attachment. It gives you the best of both worlds – reporting on a shoe string, and also control over the documents.

It's like having your own personal printing press.

How to do it...

Before we start you need to make sure that you have some data that Word is able to read. To do this, click on the Document Data Sources menu item within the Document Management folder of the Setup group within the Organization Administration area page.

You need to make sure that you have a Query Reference or a Custom Query defined for the main header table of the record that you are going to create the document template for. In this case we are creating a document template for the Sales Quotations so we have a Query Reference defined on the SalesQuotationTable table.

When you are sure that you have the query configured, click on the Close button to exit from the form.

Now open up Word and create a new Blank Document.

When the blank document is created, click on the Dynamics AX tab within the ribbon bar and then click on the Add Data button within the Design group.

This will open up the Add Data dialog box showing you all of the registered Query References and Custom Queries. Select the main Data Source that you want to use for the document template and then click the OK button.

When you return to Word you will notice that the Field Browser is now shown on the left.

Now start creating your template.

If you want to embed any field values in the word document then you can just drag and drop them from the Field Explorer over to the document.

Keep on adding fields until you have all of the field data populated.

Now save your document away.

Now that you have finished creating the template, just close down the file.

Now we need to save the document to a SharePoint Document Library. If you don't have one yet, just create a blank Document Library and then note down the URL it and then click on the Add Document link within the library.

This will open up the Upload Document dialog box. Click on the Browse button to open up the file browser.

Then navigate to the template file that you just created and click on the Open button.

When you return to the Upload Document dialog box, click on the OK button to upload the file to SharePoint.

Once you have uploaded the file, just exit out of SharePoint.

Now we need to create a Template document type that we will use to synchronize with SharePoint and then use to reference all of our document templates. To do this, click on the Document Types menu item within the Document Management folder of the Setup group within the Organization Administration area page.

When the Document Types maintenance form is displayed, click on the New button to create a new record.

Then give your new record a Type code and also a Name.

Change the Class to Template Library.

And change the Group to Document.

Then click on the folder button to the right of the Archive Directory field and point the Browser to a working directory where you can store all of the template files and then click the OK button.

You may have noticed that when you selected the Template Library Class a new tab displayed in the bottom of the form. Paste in the site URL (without the document library) for the SharePoint Document Library where you uploaded the template into the SharePoint Site field.

Then from the dropdown, select the Document Library where you stored the template.

After you have done that, click on the Synchronize button.

You should get an InfoLog box saying that one (or more) templates were synchronized.

When you return to the Document Types form you will see the Template is now shown.

All you need to do is click the Activate button to enable it.

Now when you go to your main form (the Sales Quotations in this case) and click on the Generate From Template button, the Word template will be shown to you.

When you click on it, Dynamics AX will diligently use the template that you created to create a new document instance.

And then it will open up Word for you with the template and also the key fields populated for you.

If you want to update the template for everyone, then just return to the original Word template, update it and then save it.

Then return to the SharePoint library and re-upload the template file (overwriting the previous version).

And then open up your Document Types, find the template library and click the Synchronize button again.

Dynamics AX will find the document for you and update the template it references.

If you go back to your main form and create another document from the template…

Then it will use the new version of the template that you just uploaded.

Another benefit of this feature is that all of the documents that you create are tracked and saved as attachments against the record that you created them from. To see them, just click on the Attachments button in the ribbon bar.

You will see all of the versions of the document that were created. And to see the document itself, just click on the Open button in the menu bar.

This will open up the Word document that was created by the template.

Rock on!

REPORTING TIPS

Although the standard reports that are delivered with Dynamics AX are good, you can take your own reports up to the next level by taking advantage of some of the not to visible reporting tools that are available. You can take advantage of the cubes that are delivered with Dynamics AX, you can create dashboards using Excel and PowerView, and you can even publish out data directly from Dynamics AX to Office 365 so that you all can share queries and reports.

In this section we will show some of the ways that you can create and share reports that you may not be familiar with.

Topics Covered

- Deploy The Standard Cubes For Instant Business Intelligence

- Create PowerView Dashboards Directly From Dynamics AX

- Creating PowerView Reports From Analysis Services Cubes In Excel Using PowerPivot

- Embedding PowerView Reports Into Your Role Centers

- Export PowerView Dashboards as PowerPoint To Create Dynamic Presentations

- Publish Queries As OData Document Sources For Users To Query In Excel

- Make Common Queries Available For Everyone By Saving Them To Office365

- Create Reports Instantly With Autoreports

- Export To Excel When There Is No Ribbon Bar

- Perform What-If Analysis Within Excel using PowerBI

Deploy The Standard Cubes For Instant Business Intelligence

Dynamics AX comes pre-configured with 16 reporting cubes that distills the data into a more user friendly view. You can use these to create your own reports and dashboards from, and because they remove the need to be a database expert in order to understand the data, the general users are able to take advantage of them as well.

You may think that the creation of the cubes would be an arduous task, involving a lot of design & planning, and would require weeks or even months to get them up and running, but it's not the case. All you have to do is run a simple deployment wizard and you should be up and running within minutes.

What are you waiting for?

How to do it...

From the File menu, select the Tools submenu, and then the Business Intelligence (BI) tools submenu, and select the SQL Server Analysis Services project wizard menu item.

This will start up the Analysis Services project wizard. When the welcome dialog is displayed click on the Next button.

Select the Deploy option to create a the 16 cubes from the existing project that is already built within Dynamics AX and click the Next button.

Then select the Dynamics AX product from the drop down list and click the Next button to continue.

When the Deployment options are displayed, select the data partition that you want to create the cubes for and then click the Next button.

Note: You may only have one partition.,

Also, check the Process the project after it is successfully deployed checkbox. This will process the data so that you will be able to report off it right away.

The wizard will then start running, and will probably run for a couple of minutes as the cube is being created and processed. When it is completed, just click the Next button.

Now you can exit the wizard by clicking on the Finish button.

If you look at the Analysis Services cubes within SQL Server Management Studio, you will be able to see all of the cubes that the wizard just created.

Create PowerView Dashboards Directly From Dynamics AX

If you pay attention to your Dynamics AX screens, you may notice a new button has shown up with an Analyze This label. When you see it, click on it as soon as you can because it will open up a PowerView reporting dashboard that allows you to create your own reports on the fly.

With this new tool you can create your own dashboards and reports without having to bother your IT department.

How to do it...

When you see the Analyze data button on the ribbon bar, just click on it.

This will open up a PowerView reporting canvas with all of the dimensions and measures from the standard Dynamics AX cubes.

All you need to do is build your dashboard.

Creating PowerView Reports From Analysis Services Cubes In Excel Using PowerPivot

If you have ever tried to create a PowerView report within Excel that is populated directly from an Analysis Services Cube, then you may have come across a small roadblock where PowerView refuses to work. All is not lost though, you can trick Power View into thinking that it is querying a real table by using PowerPivot to craft the query first.

The only downside to this is that we don't have to use PowerQuery as much any more...

How to do it...

Here is the problem...

Open Up Excel, and click on the Manage button within the Data Model group of the POWERPIVOT ribbon bar.

When the PowerPivot Manager is displayed, click on the Get External Data menu button and select the From Analysis Services for PowerPivot menu item.

When the Table Import Wizard dialog is displayed, specify the Server Name, and also the Database Name and then click the Next button.

Rather than write the MDX code by hand, click on the Design button when the Table Import Wizard is displayed.

When the designer is displayed, you can just drag and drop the fields over into the canvas and create your query visually. When you have completed your query, just click on the OK button.

When you return back to the initial page on the Table Import Wizard, just clock on the Finished button to complete the import.

If everything goes well, then PowerPivot will import all the records for you, and you can press the Close button.

Now within the PowerPivot Manager you will see your query directly from the Analysis Services Cubes, and you can close the form.

Now, create a PowerPivot canvas by clicking on the PowerView button within the Reports group of the Insert ribbon bar.

When the PowerView canvas is displayed, you can start adding your dimensions and measures directly from the queried cube.

With a little bit more work you end up with a great looking dashboard.

Embedding PowerView Reports Into Your Role Centers

PowerView is a great way to create your own dashboards and analysis for Dynamics AX because everyone is able to use it... even the non-technical of you out there. If you create a cool dashboard though, you don't need to keep it in the shadows of your own personal files, you can share it with others by saving it back to the PowerView reports folder, and you can also make it available to everyone by adding it to your default role centers so that everyone is able to take advantage of it.

Set your dashboards free!

How to do it...

The first thing that you need to do is to create your dashboard through PowerView.

In order to share your report, you need to save it to the server, so from the File menu, select the Save As menu item.

When the Save As dialog box is displayed, give your dashboard a File name, and then click the Save button.

To add the PowerView report to the your role center, first click on the Personalize this page link at the top right of the page.

When the role center changes to the design mode, click on the Add a Web Part link in the area that you want to add the dashboard to.

This will open up the Web Part browser, and from the Categories list, select the Microsoft Dynamics AX category, and then from the Web Parts list select the SQL Server Power View item. Then click on the Add button to insert it into your role center.

When the role center is updated, you will notice that a new SQL Server Power View panel has been added, but there is no dashboard associated with it yet.

To do this click on the small down arrow to the right of the web part name and select the Edit My Web Part menu item.

When the web part properties window shows up on the right, click on the orange table browser icon to the right of the Select a report field.

This will allow you to browse to where you saved your PowerView dashboard, and you can select and then click on the OK button.

When you return to the web part properties, you will now see that the URL for the report has been populated in the Select a report field.

Scroll down to the bottom of the properties panel and click on the OK button to save your changes.

Now when the role center is displayed, you will see your new dashboard has been embedded in the page.

To exit the design mode, just click on the Stop Editing button within the Page ribbon bar.

Now when you access your role center, you will see the new PowerView dashboard as one of the role center panels.

Export PowerView Dashboards as PowerPoint To Create Dynamic Presentations

PowerView is a great tool for creating reports and dashboards directly from Dynamics AX, and is by far one of the cooler reporting tools that you can use. It has a very cool feature that allows you to export any of your saved dashboards to PowerPoint, and these reports become interactive when you go into SlideShow mode. This is a great way to create template presentations that you can use over and over again and always have the most up-to-date data showing.

Never again will you have to create 100 variations of the same sales report where the only difference is the customer account that you are reporting on.

How to do it...

Open up the PowerView Dashboard that you want to export, and from the File menu, select the Export to PowerPoint menu item.

When PowerView notifies you that the export is complete, click on the Save button.

Now select the location and file name of the PowerPoint that you want to create and click Save.

Once the PowerPoint file has been created, you should be able to open it up and you will see a static version of the dashboard has been embedded in the slides.

You can resize the dashboard, and also add any embellishments that you may like to make the presentation prettier.

When you start the Slideshow mode, it will show the static view of the dashboard, with an Interact button in the bottom right corner, which you can click on.

If you have rights to view the dashboard interactively, you can now drill into the data through PowerPoint as if you were browsing to it the traditional way.

Publish Queries As OData Document Sources For Users To Query In Excel

If you want to publish out data to the users so that they can create their own reports, or run their own analysis, there is in a simple and secure way built into Dynamics AX. You can register your queries as Document Data Sources and then they automatically become available through the OData service within Dynamics AX. Additionally, all of the default security that you put in place around the data will be respected by the service because you are using Dynamics AX to create the query.

No more ODBC connections, or even worse... unsecured Access databases.

How to do it...

Click on the Document Data Sources menu item within the Document Management folder of the Setup group within the Organization Administration area page.

Click on the New button within the menu bar to create a new record.

Assign the Document Data Source a Module and then select the Custom query option from the Data Source Type drop down.

Now select the table or query that you want to publish as an OData Query from the Data Source Name field.

The reason why we used the Custom Query Data Source Type is because it allows us to use the Query editor to refine our results that are returned to the user. If you want to add filters you can do it here, and when you're done, just click on the OK button.

You can now rename your Data Source Name to make is a little more descriptive, and then to finish the process and make it available to the users, check the Activated checkbox.

Then click the Close button to exit from the form.

One way to access the OData query from Excel is to use PowerQuery. To do that, select the From OData Feed menu item from the From Other Sources menu button within the Get External Data group of the POWER QUERY ribbon bar.

When the OData Feed dialog box is displayed, you will want to type in the URL for Dynamics AX's OData feed service. It will probably be something similar to this:

http://servername:8101/dynamicsax/services/odataqueryservice/

When you are done, click on the OK button.

Now a Navigator Panel will show up within Excel that lists all of the available tables and queries that you can access through the OData Feed. To use it, all you need to do is click on the feed and click the Load button.

This will load the data from the feed into Power Query. To use it in Excel, just click on the Apply & Close button within the Query group of the Home ribbon bar.

Now you will have all of the data from Dynamics AX being fed directly into your worksheet.

Make Common Queries Available For Everyone By Saving Them To Office365

Queries are like mining for gold, because everyone is searching for the motherload of data that is hidden within Dynamics AX, and once they find it, they mine it until it dries out and they have to start prospecting again. Also, the secret maps to that data are hidden away, usually on someone's own personal hard drive, and are rarely shared with other prospectors. Office 365 and Power Query changes that because it allows you to share any of your queries with everyone within the organization, allowing everyone including the non-technical users that would never create a query.

No more claim jumping, there is enough data out there for everyone to mine.

How to do it...

Start off with a Query that you have created with Power Query that you want to share with everyone.

Then make sure that you are logged into Office365 via Power Query. Check on the POWER QUERY tab, and within the Organization group, there will be an icon that allows you to sign into Office 365. If it says Sign Out then you are already connected. If it says Sign In then click on it to establish a connection.

When the Power BI for Office 365 sign in dialog appears, follow the steps to sign in.

Now the connection icon should say Sign Out indicating that you are connected.

Now select your query, and then click on the Share button within the Share group of the Query ribbon bar.

When the Share Query dialog box is displayed, then you can change the Name, and add a brief Description and then click on the Share a Copy button to publish it to Office 365.

To access the query by clicking on the Online Search button within the Get External Data group of the POWER QUERY ribbon bar.

Then type in the keywords for the search in the search box. You should be able to find your query that you published and also see the sample data that was saved with the query as well. To use it, just click on the Add To Worksheet link at the bottom of the preview panel.

That will add the query to your worksheet and also refresh it with only the data that you are allowed to see.

No designing of the query required at all. How easy is that.

Create Reports Instantly With Autoreports

Sometimes you need to send someone a copy of all the data that you have on your current screen for reference. Although you can send them a screen shot, there is a much better option for you which is called an Autoreport. To create it, all you have to do is press CTRL-P and Dynamics AX will do the rest for you.

Autoreports are great because they will create reports on all of the data that you have in the query regardless of if you have multiple pages, they have hyperlinks back to the main data such as products making drilling into the information easier, and they are more secure since they can be delivered as PDF documents.

Forget the ALT-PRINTSCREEN key combination, and just remember CTRL-P.

How to do it...

From the form that you want to export out as a report, just press CTRL-P. When the Autoreport dialog box shows up click the OK button to create the report.

This will create a report for you showing exactly the same information that you had on-screen, filtered out to match the same data that you had queried.

Export To Excel When There Is No Ribbon Bar

Not all of the forms within Dynamics AX have the ribbon bar enabled with the Export to Excel icon handy for you to use when you want to gram a copy of the data, but that doesn't mean that there is no way to quickly get your data moved over to a linked worksheet.

All you need to do is select the Export to Microsoft Excel menu item from the Files menu, or for those of you that love shortcut keys, just press CTRL+T and Dynamics AX will create an Excel Workbook with all of the data from the form populated in it.

How to do it...

Select the Export to Microsoft Excel menu item from the Files menu.

Note: Your can also just press CTRL+T if you like using keyboard shortcuts.

Now all of the data in the current form will be exported to a new Excel workbook.

Perform What-If Analysis Within Excel using PowerBI

Sometimes you want to have a way to juggle numbers a little to perform quick what-if analysis, but you are not committed to the change at the time so you really don't want to be changing the codes within Dynamics AX just yet, and would rather have the changes remain off-line until some time in the future.

In this example we will show you how to use an off-line worksheet that contains all of the changes that you want to make along with PowerPivot and PowerView to create a simple dashboard to track the impact that changes would have on your data.

How to do it...

Before we start we will need some data to analyze. For this example we will get the backordered sales information. We made one small personalization change to the default form, and that was to add in the Customer Group, Sales Group, and Sales District for analysis

We then just exported this information to Excel.

We will also need a worksheet that stores all of our alternate codings that we want to use for our What-If scenarios. Here we created a table that lists out all of the customers and their proposed groupings.

Once we have our Excel workbook with the linked data that we want to analyze, we will add it to a PowerPivot model by clicking on the Add to Data Model button within the Tables group of the POWERPIVOT ribbon bar.

When the PowerPivot Manager window is displayed, click on the From Other Sources button within the Get External Data group of the Home ribbon bar, and select the Excel File option so that we can link in our What-If mappings.

After choosing the worksheet that we created with the mew mappings, the data from the worksheet will be linked in with the PowerPivot model.

There is one last step that we need to perform here, and that is to link the tables. To do this, click on the Diagram View option within the View group of the Home ribbon bar and when the two tables are displayed, link them based off the Customer account. Now you can close out of the PowerPivot Manager.

Now we can return to the Excel worksheet and create a new PowerView report based of the data by clicking on the PowerView menu item within the Reports group of the Insert ribbon bar.

When the reporting canvas is displayed, you will be able to create a simple analysis based on the main (real) table data within the worksheet.

And you can create a second set of dashboard elements showing the data, but using the classifications that you have defined in the off-line worksheet.

The great thing about this is that you can change the What-If classifications within the off-line worksheet...

And if you click the Refresh button within the PowerView ribbon bar, the data will instantly change in the PowerView dashboard.

WORKFLOW TRICKS

Workflow is one of the most misunderstood areas of Dynamics AX, mainly because people think that it's complicated, and requires a developer to set it up and make it work properly. That is far from the case. A lot of the things that you can do with Workflow don't require you to write a single line of come, but add so much accountability to the users and the processes in the system.

In this section we will show some of the ways that you can use the Workflows to streamline your business processes.

Topics Covered

- Set Up A Workflow Delegate When You Are Not Available

- Use Workflow Escalation To Make Sure Tasks Get Done

- Use Workflows Escalation Automatic Approval For Spot Reviews

- Allow Multiple People To Be Involved In Workflow Approval Steps

- Create Multiple Versions Of Workflows And Choose When To Use Them

- Add Workflow Feedback Loops To Check Tasks Are Performed

- Use Workflows To Trap Transactions For Particular Accounts For Review

- Streamline Your Workflows By Automatically Performing Tasks Based On Conditions

Set Up A Workflow Delegate When You Are Not Available

Workflow is a great way to assign tasks to people and then track the progress of the tasks, because they are always visible, and never get misplaced or lost like the manual processes tend to allow. But sometimes you just have to take a break, and rather than having your workflow tasks languish until you get back, or even worse, follow you on vacation, use the delegation feature within Dynamics AX to route them to someone else that you trust.

Now you can sleep at night knowing that someone else is doing your work.

How to do it...

From the File menu, select the Tools submenu, and then click on the Options menu item.

When the Options dialog box is displayed, change the tab group to Delegation, and then click on the Add button within the menu bar.

Now just say who you want to delegate all of your workflows to, set a from and to date, and then set it to be Enabled.

Dynamics AX will now route all of the workflows to your delegate.

Use Workflow Escalation To Make Sure Tasks Get Done

Workflows are great, because they allow you to control your business processes in a more efficient way than the traditional paper (or even worse word of mouth) and make sure that tasks don't get lost or forgotten. If you want to make them even more efficient then you can implement escalation rules that will assign tasks up the reporting chain when they are not done in a timely manner.

Like cream, workflow tasks can also float to the top...

How to do it...

Open up your workflow design, and navigate to the element that you want to add the escalation rule to, and then then click on the Assignment button within the Modify Step group of the Workflow ribbon bar.

When the workflow step properties dialog box is displayed, select the Time Limit tab from the Assignment group, and set the expected time that you want the task to be performed within.

Now switch to the Escalation group, and check the Use Escalation Path checkbox to enable escalations.

The Escalation tab will now expand to show you a number of new options that are used to define your Escalation Path.

Click on the Add Escalation button within the Escalation tab to add your first person in the escalation process.

To escalate to another user, select the User option from the Assignment Type sub-tab.

Switch to the User sub-tab, and select the user that you want to be notified when the original task has not been completed.

You can then switch to the Time Limit sub-tab as well if you want to adjust the time that is allotted for that user to act upon the escalated task.

To complete the setup, select the Action item which is added by default to all escalation paths, and from the dropdown list, select the action that is to be performed when all escalations fail. In most cases the best choice is to err on the cautious side and select the Reject option.

After you have finished, you can click the Close button and activate the workflow.

Now when the workflow is processed, people will be motivated to act upon them ASAP.

Use Workflows Escalation Automatic Approval For Spot Reviews

You may think that the escalation rules can just be used to move a task up the corporate ladder when someone fails to pull their weight, but there is a kinder side of their nature as well. You can configure them to automatically approve tasks as well if they are not acted upon, making them a great way to have tasks assigned to users for review, but if they don't have the time to act upon them, or if they just want to periodically review transactions, then the tasks that they do not look at will continue on their merry way through the workflow.

It's just like throwing a D20 to see if your workflow is reviewed.

How to do it...

Open up your workflow design, and navigate to the element that you want to add the escalation rule to, and then then click on the Assignment button within the Modify Step group of the Workflow ribbon bar.

When the workflow step properties dialog box is displayed, select the Time Limit tab from the Assignment group, and set the time that you want task to be available for approval.

Now switch to the Escalation group, and check the Use Escalation Path checkbox to enable escalations.

In this case, don't assign any more people to the escalation path, but select the Action line within the escalation rule, and set it to Approve.

After you have finished, you can click the Close button and activate the workflow.

Now when the workflow is processed, the user that is assigned the task will have a set amount of time to review the transaction, and then if they do not act upon the task, then it will continue to the next step in the workflow.

Allow Multiple People To Be Involved In Workflow Approval Steps

Not all decisions are made by just one person, there are a lot of times where you need to get multiple people involved as an internal check policy, or maybe you just love making decisions as a group and don't want to leave anyone out. Doing this through workflow within Dynamics AX is a synch as well, because you can include as many people in a single decision process as you like and have them weigh in during the workflow execution. There are also a lot of different ways that you can allow the votes to be counted to speed up the process as well.

Everything is better when it's decided by committee... right?

How to do it...

Select the workflow step that you want to allow multiple people to approve and click on the Assignment button within the Modify Step group of the Workflow ribbon bar.

When the Assignment properties are displayed, click on the User tab and add all of the people that you want involved in the workflow step to the Selected Users side of the selection box.

Then switch to the Completion Policy tab.

If you select the Single Approver option, then as soon as one of the approvers either approves or declines this step then the task will be marked as completed.

If you select the Majority of Approvers option then you need to have a majority of the users to approve or decline the task before it will continue on. Not all users necessarily have to weigh in.

Note: make sure that you have the numbers for a majority vote so that you don't end up with a hung jury.

If you select the Percentage of Approvers option you will be allowed to fill in a % value. This is similar to the Majority of approvers option, except you define the watermark to get the step completed.

Finally, if you select the All Approvers then all of the people that you selected in the list must approve this task before it continues on.

Once you have selected your completion policy then you can click the close button and your approval step will be updated.

Create Multiple Versions Of Workflows And Choose When To Use Them

Workflows are great, but there are a lot of times that you want to run one version of the workflow in this situation, and another version of the workflow in a different situation. You could take the Sauron approach and create one workflow to rule them all, and embed in conditional tree at the beginning of the workflow that routes you to the right decision tree, or you can just create multiple workflows, and then use the Activation option to tell Dynamics AX when to use the variations of your workflows.

Now you can create an army of workflows that are all unique.

How to do it...

Start off by creating the different workflow processes that you want to use. In this case we have a couple of Case Management workflows that we want to process in different scenarios.

Open up the workflow, and then click on the Properties menu button within the Show group of the Workflow ribbon bar.

When the Properties maintenance form is displayed, click on the Activation group on the left hand side.

Check the Set the Condition For Running The Workflow check box, to enable the Activation Conditions details to be displayed, and then click on the Add Condition button.

This will create a new condition line where you can select any field element from the Case and also any comparison that you may want to write.

In this case we activate the case only when it is a New Product Request, and then save and activate the workflow.

Repeat the process for all of the other workflows.

In this second workflow, we will only run this when it's a Customer Issue, and then close out of the workflow editor.

Now when we open up the case, based on the activation rules that we have enabled for the workflow it will pick and choose which one to run.

For Customer Issues, we will run the Customer Issue workflow.

For New Product Requests we will run the New Production Request workflow.

Even the submission instructions will be tailored to the type of workflow that you are about to run.

How cool is that?

Add Workflow Feedback Loops To Check Tasks Are Performed

Workflows are great because they automate the assignment of tasks to the right people at the right time like a well-oiled machine. The only thing that they cannot control is that the people actually do the work that they have been asked to do though. If you have bugs within your people processes, then you can add feedback loops into your workflows though that allow you to make sure that all of the fields that you ask the users to update have actually been updated.

Now a failing grade on the task will be caught right away.

How to do it...

Start off by opening up your workflow within the editor. If this case we have a customer issue case workflow where we are asking someone to assign the task to a user.

To add a feedback loop, drag the Conditional Decision workflow element onto the workflow canvas, and then click on the Basic Settings button within the Modify group of the Workflow ribbon bar.

When the Conditional Decision properties are displayed, click on the Add Condition button within the Condition tab.

When the new condition is added, click on the field browser and select the field that you want to validate has been updates.

In this case it's the Case.Employee Responsible field.

Now change the condition to be true when the field is not empty.

All that is left now is to link up the condition so that when the task is completed, if the field has not been updated, then the workflow returns to the previous task.

Use Workflows To Trap Transactions For Particular Accounts For Review

Although you always want to keep an eye on the transactions that are flowing through Dynamics AX, sometimes there are transactions that you want to keep an even closer eye on. Workflow is a great way to do this, but maybe you don't want to have to initiate a workflow for every transaction, maybe you just want to do it in certain situations. Not a problem, you can tell Dynamics AX when to run the workflow, and in all other cases don't even show the submit button.

It's a devilishly fiendish way to trap transactions.

How to do it...

Start off by creating a simple approval workflow.

Then click on the Basic Settings within the Modify group of the Workflow ribbon bar, and select the Activation tab.

Check the Set the conditions for running the workflow flag to enable the Activation Condition group, and then click on the Add Condition button,

Configure the Condition that you want to perform the workflow for, and then click the Close button to exit from the form.

Note: In this case we are just going to check for one vendor that we want to keep a closer eye on.

Now when we select a PO for any other vendor than the one that we set the trap for, everything looks normal.

But for our problem Vendor we have to run through an approval workflow before we can confirm the PO.

Then workflow notifications will start popping up all over the place.

Streamline Your Workflows By Automatically Performing Tasks Based On Conditions

Workflows are great because they enforce a uniform procedure to your business processes, and make sure people are not sidestepping the standard procedures through creative approval processes. But that doesn't mean that you can't build steps into your workflows that are sidestepped in certain situations. If you don't want a certain task to be performed based on a dollar value, or a coding on the record, then you can use the conditional processing on the workflow tasks to automatically complete it and then continue on to the next step in the workflow.

This way you will always have the users wondering if they are going to have to do something else, or get a free pass through the workflow.

How to do it...

Start off by opening up your workflow that you want to streamline, select the task that you want to make conditional and then click on the Automatic Actions button within the Modify Element group of the Workflow ribbon bar.

When the Properties maintenance form is displayed, check the Enable Automatic Actions flag within the Automatic Actions page.

This will enable the condition designer, and you can then click on the Add Condition button.

When the condition line is displayed, click on the field box and select the field for the related table that you want to use as your condition.

And then specify the rest of the condition clause.

Finally, select the Auto Complete Action that you want to perform when the condition is true.

Note: notice that you don't just have to approve the task, you can also automatically reject the task as well.

Once you have completed the change, then just exit out of the workflow and save the changes.

Now if we run through the task that the workflow is related to and the condition is not met everything looks like normal and we have to perform the workflow task.

But if the condition is met then the task is skipped.

If we look at the workflow history then we will see that the action was automatically performed.

How cool is that?

SYSTEM ADMINISTRATION TIPS

There are a lot of wizards and tools that are included with Dynamics AX that are designed to make the administration and management of the system easier, but they are not there just for the System Administrator, everyone is able to take advantage of them. Features like Alerts, and tools like the Task Recorder are invaluable to everyone.

In this section we will show a few examples of how you can use these administrative tools to save time and make your life generally better.

Topics Covered

- Let Alerts Watch For Changes To Your Favorite Data

- Use The New Task Recorder To Create Training Documents And Videos

- Use Your Own Personalized Template When Creating Documents From The Task Recorder

- Document Regulations & Requirements Within The Compliance Portal

- Link Task Recordings As Evidence Of Internal Controls Within The Compliance Portal

- Save Time By Saving Task Recordings Directly To Compliance Process Documentation Library

- Archive Excel Exports Automatically In SharePoint Document Libraries

- Share Your Screen Personalization With Other Users

- Archive Reports So That You Can Access Then Later On Without Rerunning It

- Save Document Attachments To SharePoint

- Creating Segregation Of Duties Rules To Block Possible Security Issues

- Hide The Parent Navigation Tabs To Tidy Up The Portal Navigation Bar

- Add SharePoint Documents Libraries As Menu Links

- Copy Data From One Partition To Another Using The Data Import Export

- Assign User Permissions through Active Directory Groups

- Restrict User Access To Certain Companies Through Roles

- Import Data Using The Data Import Export Framework

- Restrict Field Access By Security Role

- Copy Data Between Companies Quickly Using The Data Import Export Framework

- Add Quick Links To Websites As Ribbon Bar Buttons

- Deliver Blog Feeds Directly To Your Role Centers

- Make Users Feel Special By Creating New Role Centers For Their Unique Roles

- Add Flair To Your Forms With Achievements

- Choose Where To Go When You Click On Pop-Up Notifications

- Declutter Your System By Turning Off License Features You Don't Use

- Add Menu Items To The Tools Menu

- Create Composite Menus That Combine Functions From Multiple Areas

Let Alerts Watch For Changes To Your Favorite Data

Everyone has a little bit of data within Dynamics AX that they are especially attached to and would rather that other people not tinker with because it would throw a spanner into their finely oiled routines. Rather than continually looking over your shoulder and rechecking the data, or even worse waiting for someone to change the data and then be sent into a tailspin days later, you can add alerts to your precious fields that will notify you immediately when a change is made to a field, and you can track down and fix the data right away.

Alerts are your own personal Informants within Dynamics AX.

How to do it...

Right-mouse-click on the field that you want to track the changes on, and select the Create alert rule... menu item from the pop up menu.

When the Create alert rule dialog box is displayed, you can change any of the default configurations of the alert to allow you to track the entire tables, just this particular record, add a custom message, and also change who is being alerted, and even send the alert to an e-mail address.

In most cases, you can just click on the OK button and accept the defaults.

Dynamics AX will then show you all of the Alerts that you have configured. Just click the Close button to exit out of the form and return to the main form you started at.

To see the Alert in action, just change the field that you created the alert for.

You will receive notifications through the Notifications List and also through pop-up toast card.

Clicking on the Notification will show you the change that was made, and when the change was made.

If you click on the Go to Origin menu item in the Notification List form then it will take you straight to the record that was changed.

Use The New Task Recorder To Create Training Documents And Videos

The Task Recorder has always been a great tool for creating user training documentation, but with the CU6/7 releases of Dynamics AX, it has been taken to the next level. When you create your task recordings, it now automatically creates your task recording documents for you so that you don't have to do that step manually, and also it creates a recording of your Task Recording automatically.

This makes the generation of training martial, and reference videos a breeze.

How to do it...

From the Files menu click on the Tools menu item, and select the Task Recorder submenu.

When the Task Recorder opens, select the node in your Framework Hierarchy that you want to record the training material for, and click on the Start button within the Record group of the Record ribbon bar.

Then perform the task.

When you have finished the task, return to the Task Recorder and click the Stop button within the Record group of the Record ribbon bar.

To find where all of your recording documents are being stored, click on the Parameters button within the Setup group of the Settings ribbon bar of the Task Recorder.

Note down the part that is being used for the Recording File Path.

If you navigate to the Recording File Path location within the file explorer, then you will notice that there are folders for all of the Task Recordings that you have made, including the one that you just did.

If you click on the .doc version, then you will see the Word version of the task recording.

If you click on the .wmv version, then you will see a recording of everything that you did in real time.

Use Your Own Personalized Template When Creating Documents From The Task Recorder

The task recorder is great because it practically creates all of your user documentation for you. The only problem is that the format of the documentation that it created is a little bland. Don't worry though, rather than reformat all of the documents that are created after the fact, you have the option to change the default template that is used when the documents are created.

An ounce of preparation is worth a pound of cure

How to do it...

First we need to find where the templates are stored that Task Recorder uses when creating the documents. To do this click on the Parameters button within the Setup group of the Settings ribbon bar of the task recorder. You will be able to see the file location in the Template File Path field.

Locate the Task Recorder Templates folder within the file explorer and open the Task Recorder template.dotx template file.

This will open up the default template that the Task Recorder uses when creating the recording transcripts.

You can now reformat the template and change the headings.

If you want to add some information to the footers then you can do that as well.

You can also add additional pages to the document template that will always be included when the document is created. This is a great way to add your company specific disclaimers, or notes and links that you always want shown on the document.

When you have finished, save the template.

You can see the new template in action by opening up the Task Recorder, finding a business process that you have recorded, and then click on the Document menu item within the Manage group of the Record ribbon bar.

The document that is created will now use your new default template, saving you a lot of time in reformatting.

Document Regulations & Requirements Within The Compliance Portal

Dynamics AX is delivered with a Compliance Portal that is designed to help you manage and track all of your procedures, policies, risks and compliance documentation within a shared and secure location. It allows you to document all of this information, track the approval workflows, and also link supporting documentation for auditing and future reference.

Documenting compliance is a thankless and time consuming job, but it doesn't have to be a disorganized one.

How to do it...

To start tracking your compliance documentation, open up the Compliance Portal and then click on the Internal Controls menu item within the Internal Controls menu group.

To create a new document, just click on the Add Document menu button within the Internal Controls ribbon bar.

When the Create document dialog box is displayed, give your document a name, and then also choose a template that you want to use in order to manage the approval process.

When you have done that, just click on the Create and Exit button to create the compliance document entry.

This will take you into the document detail where you can add additional control data on your document.

If you want to associate supporting documentation, then you can scroll down to the bottom of the page, and click on the Add evidence via URL link within the Evidence group.

This will allow you to link a web page to this document.

When you are done, just click on the Save button to exit the form.

Now you will have a entry for your compliance procedure, risk, or issue.

Link Task Recordings As Evidence Of Internal Controls Within The Compliance Portal

Task Recordings are a great way to create documentation to support your compliance processes because all of the hard work with the document generation is done for you. But you can make them even more useful by attaching them directly to your compliance processes within the Compliance Portal as supporting evidence that all required tests were performed.

The next time an Auditor asks you to provide more information, ask them if they have seen the movie... the Task Recording movie that is.

How to do it...

Before you start, copy over your task recordings into the Process Documentation library within the Compliance Portal.

Select the Internal Controls menu item within the Internal Controls group of the Compliance Portal.

When the Internal Controls hierarchy is shown, select the node that you want to associate the task recording with and then click on the Edit button within the Internal Controls ribbon bar.

When the document is displayed, scroll down to the bottom and click on the Add evidence from process documentation link within the Evidence group.

This will open up a list box that will allow you to search through all of the documents that you have stored away within the Process Documentation library. You can select the task recording document that you want to associate with the control document and then just click the Add button.

You can repeat this process by adding as many task recordings as you like.

Now everything is filed away.

Save Time By Saving Task Recordings Directly To Compliance Process Documentation Library

If you are using the Task Recorder to document policies and procedures and then attaching them to your Internal Controls within the Compliance Portal then you may want to set up the Task Recorder to automatically save to the library by default, so that you don't have to manually copy them there.

With all this new spare time, you won't know what to do with yourself.

How to do it...

Open up the Process Documentation document list within the Compliance Portal and click on the Open In Explorer icon within the Connect & Export group of the Library ribbon bar.

This will open up the library within Explorer. Now click on the Easy Access menu button, and select the Map as Drive option.

When the Map Network Drive dialog box appears, select a Drive Letter that is not currently in use, and then click the Finish button.

This will open up the document library again, but this time it will be referenced by the drive letter that you assigned it.

Now, open up the Task Recorder and click on the Parameters menu item within the Setup group of the Settings ribbon bar.

When the Task Recorder Parameters dialog box is displayed, change the Recording File Path to point to your mapped drive.

Now just record a task.

If you check out the mapped drive you will find that the recording is now stored there.

And if you browse to the Process Documents library within the Compliance Portal then you will find that the Task Recording files are available for you to reference.

What a time saver!

Archive Excel Exports Automatically In SharePoint Document Libraries

When you export data from Excel, by default it creates a temporary export file locally on your workstation, although there is an option that you can use that will allow you to automatically archive the export to a default directory. This has the added benefit that you are also able to archive the files then to SharePoint. If you would like to make your exports sharable, or would just like to have a place to go to see all of the exports that you have done in the past, then this is a great option to configure.

You're not a data packrat if you do this...

How to do it...

First, start off by creating a document library within SharePoint where you would like to archive off all of your exported files.

Then select the Tools menu item from the Options submenu of the Files menu.

Expand the Miscellaneous tab group and paste in the URL for your document library into the Export Location field. Make sure that you have the "/" on the end of the file path or else Dynamics AX will complain a little.

To see this in action, just export any data to Excel.

Your export will work exactly the same way as it did before...

Although it will now use SharePoint as the archive for all of the documents.

And also you will be able to see all of the version history of the document, including any changes that the user made when they manipulated the data... if you have version control turned on of course.

Share Your Screen Personalization With Other Users

If you have ever had a situation where another user has perfected the exact screen layout, and you want to use that same layout yourself, but don't have the time to personalize the forms, then don't worry. If you ask the user nicely they can save away that layout for you, and then you can apply it to your screens in a heartbeat through the personalization options.

Imitation is the sincerest form of flattery.

How to do it...

On the form that you want to share, right-mouse-click in the body, and select the Personalize option.

When the Personalization dialog box is displayed click on the Save button on the far right of the form.

This will open up a Save user setup dialog box where you can give your saved screen layout a name and then click on the Close button.

If a user likes you screen layout, and wants to quickly load the same configuration, all they need to do is open up the same form and then right-mouse-click on the body of the form so that the context menu is displayed. Then they need to select the Personalize menu item.

When the Personalization dialog box is displayed, they then should click the Retrieve from user button on the far right.

This will display a list of users that have saved their configurations that they can double click on.

And then they will be asked which configuration they would like to copy (you can have multiple versions saved away).

The next time that they open up the form, they will have the same format as the user that they copied the configuration from.

Archive Reports So That You Can Access Then Later On Without Rerunning It

When you rerun a report, there is a small chance that you will get slightly different report, because flags have been changed, or the report has been modified. If you want to preserve your report as it was when it was originally ran, then you can easily do that by saving it to the Report Archive. Once the report is archived, you can return to it over and over again without even rerunning it.

Now you have your very own microfiche system – minus the clunky reader.

How to do it...

When you print any document, you may have noticed that there is a Save in Print Archive checkbox. To save the report to access later on, just check the box.

Also, if you always want to archive the documents, then you can set this as a default option within the Print Management

To view all of the archived documents, just click on the Files menu, select the Tools submenu, and then click on the Print Archive menu item.

This will show you a list of all the reports that you have archived. To view the report, all you need to do is click on the Print Preview button within the menu bar.

Then you will be able to see the original report.

Save Document Attachments To SharePoint

The document attachments function within Dynamics AX is super useful, but if you don't want all of the files that you attach cluttering up your database, or stored away on a local file share, there is another option available. You can save them off to SharePoint. This also has a side benefit of allowing you to take advantage of the features of SharePoint such as document control, versioning, and also workflow if you like to manage the processing of the attached documents.

How to do it...

Before you start, make sure that you have a document library within SharePoint that you can save your documents to.

The next step is to configure the Document Types so that they point to the SharePoint document library. To do that, click on the Document Types menu item within the Document Management folder of the Setup group within the Organization Administration area page.

When the Document Types maintenance form is displayed, find the Document Type that you want to save to SharePoint, set the Location field to SharePoint and then paste in the URL for your SharePoint library into the Archive Directory field.

Now if you add a file as an attachment using that Document Type, it will save it to SharePoint, giving you a reference location for it in the notes.

If you open up the SharePoint document library, you will see the file has been safely archived for you.

Creating Segregation Of Duties Rules To Block Possible Security Issues

There are two approaches to security that most people adhere to, the Lord Of The Fly's approach, or the 1984 approach. The first is where there is no security and the users will police themselves, and the second is where everything is controlled and monitored because the users cannot be trusted.

If you are in the latter camp when it comes to security, then you can even secure the security managers by implementing security rules that manage the security managers themselves through the Segregation of Duties functions within Dynamics AX.

How to do it...

From the System Administration area page, click on the Segregation of duties rules menu item within the Segregation of Duties subfolder within the Security folder of the Setup group.

When the Segregation of Duties Rules maintenance form is displayed, click on the New button in the menu bat to create a new rule.

Then give your rule a Name and then select the First Duty for the rule.

Then select the Second Duty that you do not want the users to have if they also have the first.

If you want, you can also assign a Severity level to the rule, because some infractions are not as serious as others.

When you are done, just click the Close button to exit from the form.

Now if anyone tries to tinker with the security and assign roles that give them questionable rights they will be notified of the conflict right away.

Now the watchers are being watched.

Hide The Parent Navigation Tabs To Tidy Up The Portal Navigation Bar

When you install the Enterprise Portals, by default, all of the sites are displayed within the navigation bar. This is OK if you only have a couple installed, but if you have them all up and running, and then start to create collaboration workspaces, the top navigation pane can quickly start chewing up your screen real-estate, and more importantly make the screen look untidy.

Luckily, since this is built on SharePoint, you can easily change the default settings so that you just see the current portal name in the navigation bar, an everything looks so much cleaner.

How to do it...

Philip K. Dicks Law of Kipple in action...

Click on the Site Actions menu item, and select the Site Settings menu item.

When the Site Settings menu is displayed, click on the Navigation menu item from within the Look and Feel menu group.

When the Navigation Settings options page is displayed, check the Display the navigation items below the current site radio button within the Global Navigation group and then click OK to save the preferences.

Now when you return to your portal, you will not see all of the other sites cluttering up your navigation bar.

Add SharePoint Documents Libraries As Menu Links

Storing documents within SharePoint is cool. It allows you to browse through the documents, it allows you to have version control, it allows you to add metadata that you can use to search for documents, it does everything. The problem is that if you work in the AX client all the time, then you have to switch out of the application in order to view all the related documents. Don't worry. If you want to access all of the documents from within Dynamics AX then you can add it to the menu.

Now all of the Axoraphobiacs out there don't have to leave the application all day.

How to do it...

First, start off by finding your document library within SharePoint and note down the URL for the document library.

And then find the location where you want to put your link to the Documents...

The first step is to create a form that will show the Documents. To do that, open up a new development environment (CTRL+D) right-mouse-click on the Forms group, and select the New Form menu item.

When the new form is created, change the Name in the Properties to something a little more friendly.

Now we need to add a web browser control to the form. To do that expand out the form details, and expand the Designs group.

Then right mouse click on the Design design click on the New Control submenu, and select the ActiveX menu item.

When the ActiveX browser is displayed, scroll down and select the Microsoft Web Browser control and click on the OK button.

Now you should see that the ActiveX control has been added to the form design.

Change the Width property to Column Width and the Height property to Column Height so that it will expand to take up all of the real-estate in the form.

Now we need to make sure that the browser points to our document management library. To do that right-mouse-click on the Methods group, select the Override method menu and click on the Activate method in the sub-menu.

Then add the following lines to the body:

```
String255
url="http://intranet.contoso.com/documents/AP%20Invoices/For
ms/AllItems.aspx?isdlg=1";
```

```
ActiveX.Navigate(url);
```

Notice that the URL is just the URL to the document library.

Now we need to add a menu item to open up the form. To do this, expand the Menu Items group, and then right-mouse-click on the Display subfolder and select the New Menu Item menu item.

When the new menu item is displayed, give it a more appropriate Name and Label, and then select the new form that you just created from the Object drop down.

Also, set the RunOn property to Client.

Finally we now need to add the menu item to a menu. To do that, open up the Menus group, and expand the menu that you want to modify (in this case the AccountsPayable).

Right-mouse-click on the menu, and New menu and select the Submenu option.

This will create a new submenu group for you that you can call Documents.

Then right-mouse-click on that submenu, and select the New menu, and this time select the Menu Item option.

When the menu item is displayed, change the MenuItemName to be the form that you initially created.

Then save your changes and exit from the development environment.

Now when you open up your menu there will be a new link there for your document library...

And clicking on it will open up your document library within the Dynamics AX client.

How cool is that.

Copy Data From One Partition To Another Using The Data Import Export

Creating new partitions is a great way to create new instances of Dynamics AX without the overhead of creating new databases, and installing new AOS servers, because it piggybacks on the existing infrastructure you have. But it also means that you need to set up all of the data in the partition because it start's off as a blank system... or do you? Dynamics AX has an inbuilt export and import function that allows you to export out all of the data in one partition and then import it into another.

Duplication has never been so easy.

How to do it...

The first step in the process is to create an export from your original database partition. To do this click on the Definition Groups menu item within the Data Export/Import folder of the Common group within the System Administration area page.

When the Definition Groups maintenance form is displayed, click on the New button within the menu bar to create a new record.

When the Create Table Definition Group dialog box is displayed, assign your record a Definition Group code and Description.

Then switch to the Include Table Groups tab within the dialog box. This will show you all of the different types of data that you want to export. By default all of the codes and controls are marked to be exported, which would allow you to create a export template for a new company partition.

In this case though we will select all of the table groups so that we can export the entire database and all of the transactions.

When you have selected the table groups that you want to export, just click the OK button to finish the setup.

Now we can create an export file. To do this, click on the Export button within the menu bar of the Definition Groups maintenance form.

When the Export Options dialog box is displayed, click on the folder icon to the right of the File Name field and define a new file and location for the export.

Also, select the File Type of export that you want to perform. This can either be Comma for simple exports, or Binary for when you have a database that you want to retain carriage returns etc. in the data.

Now just wait for the export to complete.

After the export has completed, you should see a .dat, and .def file within you export folder containing all of the information from the company.

Now we can import all of the data into our empty target partition. To do that open up the target partition, and then create a definition group that matches the one that we used within the source database for the export.

Then click on the Import button within the menu bar of the Definition Groups maintenance form, point the File Name to your file that you created during the export, and click on the OK button.

The import will first analyze the data within the export file and check for possible problems.

You may get a couple of dialog boxes that indicate that there are fields or parameters that don't exist in the target database, buy just throw caution to the wind, and click on the Yes button.

Also the Import will ask you if you want to clean out some of the tables. Don't select any of them, because Dynamics AX will merge the data in the common tables like UOM etc. for you. Continue by clicking on the OK button.

When the merge confirmation box is displayed, click on the Yes button.

Then just let Dynamics AX do all of the hard work for you.

When it finishes you will see all of your data is now set up in your new partition.

That was a way simpler way to load a demo within R3 than I was originally thinking that I would have to do it ☺

Assign User Permissions through Active Directory Groups

Access to all of the roles have to be configured within Dynamics AX, but that does not mean that all of the users have to be managed there as well. If you want, you can link all of the security roles to Active Directory Groups, and then within Active Directory, when you assign the users to the groups, then Dynamics AX will automatically inherit these, even if the user is not explicitly added to the system.

Now you can manage all security access through Active Directory and simplify your security administrators life.

How to do it...

First create a new user group within Active Directory

Then assign your user to the Active Directory Group.

To add the Active Directory Group to the Dynamics AX users, click on the Users menu item within the Users folder of the Common group within the System Administration area page.

When the Users maintenance form is displayed, click on the User menu button within the New group of the Users ribbon bar.

Give your new User record a User ID, set the User Name, Network Domain, and Alias to match the security group that you created within Active Directory and then change the Account Type to be Active Directory User.

Then click the Assign Roles menu button within the User Roles tab to link your security roles with the group.

When the Assign Roles To User dialog box is displayed, select the user roles that you want associated with the group and then click on the OK button to assign them to the user group.

Finally, check the Enabled checkbox on the user group and then click on the Close button to exit the form.

Now if you log into Dynamics AX using the user that you assigned to the user group within Active Directory they will inherit the security roles of the group, even though they have not been explicitly set up within Dynamics AX as a user.

How easy is that!

Restrict User Access To Certain Companies Through Roles

The multi-company capability within Dynamics AX is one of the major selling points of the application, because you can easily switch between organizations with just a click of a button. But that does not mean that you want everyone to have free reign to perform transactions in any company, or even to see some of the other company data. If you want to simplify the users choices just to one or more select companies then that's not a problem though, you can do that easily through the user administration.

It's like putting your users on house arrest.

How to do it...

Start off by finding the user that you want to restrict access to just a select number of companies.

Now open up the user profile, and click on the Assign Organizations menu button within the User's Roles tab.

When the Organizations for the User * maintenance form is displayed, you will see that the user has full access to all of the companies within the system.

To restrict access, click on the Grant Access o Specific Organizations Individually radio button.

This will allow you to select from the Available Organization Nodes. Select Organization that you want to grant the user access to, and then click on the Grant button.

You can repeat this process for any additional Organizations that you want them to have access to and then click on the Close button to exit the form.

The next time the user logs in, they will only see the organization that you have granted them access to.

Import Data Using The Data Import Export Framework

Although Excel is a great way to import base data into Dynamics AX, sometime you need to bring in the big guns and that's where the Data Import Export Framework applies. This is a new module that makes importing data into Dynamics AX so much simpler, especially when importing complex data types that include multiple dependent tables. All you need to do is check the data that you want to import and the D.I.E.F. will do the rest for you.

On a side note, "dief" in Dutch actually means "thief". Is this a coincidence, or is it a reminder that the D.I.E.F. stealing data seem so simple?

How to do it...

First we need to make sure that the Data Import Export Framework is configured. To do this, click on the Data Import/Export Framework Parameters menu item within the Setup group of the Data Import Export Framework area page.

When the Data Import/Export Framework Parameters maintenance form is displayed, make sure that you have a Shared Working Directory has been defined. If you don't have one yet, just specify a working directory, and then click on the Validate button to make sure that you have the correct access to the folder.

Then click on the Close button to exit from the form.

Next we need to make sure that we have a data format defined that we will be using for our import files. To do that, click on the Source Data Format menu item within the Setup group of the Data Import Export Framework area page.

When the Source Data Formats maintenance form is displayed, make sure that you have some import formats defined. In this case we have a CSV format defined.

If you have not got any formats defined ye, just click on the New button in the menu bar to create a new record and specify your import preferences.

After you have configured your import format then just click on the Close button to exit from the form.

Now we can start importing data. To do that, just click on the Processing Group menu item within the Common group of the Data Import Export Framework area page.

When the Processing Group maintenance form is displayed, click the New button in the menu bar to create a new record, and then assign your record a Group Name and Description.

Once you have created your new Processing Group, click on the Entities button within the menu bar to start adding your import entities to your Processing Group.

When the Select Entities For Processing Group maintenance form is displayed, click on the New button in the menu bar to create a new record, and then from the Entity dropdown, select he type of data you want to import – in this case we will import products.

Then select the Source Data Format that you want to use for the import.

Next we need to specify the data that we want to import. To do this click on the Generate Source File button within the menu bar.

This will start up a wizard to guide you through the process. Click on the Next button to start the process.

When the Display Data page of the wizard is displayed, you can select any of the fields that have been mapped to your Entity, and also rearrange the order to your liking.

Once you have chosen all of the fields that you want, click on the Generate Sample File button.

This will create a new blank template for you based on the Source Data Format that you chose.

Save the file away to a working folder, we will need this in a second.

When you return to the Select Entities For Processing Group maintenance form, point the Sample File Path to point to the sample file that you just created.

Now we need to link all of the fields that we chose to import to all of the actual entities. To do that, click on the Generate Source Mapping button within the menu bar.

This should result in a pretty uneventful message saying that the mapping was successful.

If you click on the Modify Source Mapping button in the menu bar, then you will see what Dynamics AX has really done – link all of the source fields to the import staging table.

If you want to make doubly sure that everything is working, then click on the Validate button within the menu bar and you should have no errors.

Now open up the sample import file that you created.

All you need to do is paste in all of your data and save the file.

Now you can preview the data that you put in the import file by clicking on the Preview Source File menu button within the Select Entities For Processing Group maintenance form.

In the Preview area you will be able to see all of the data.

Click on the Close button to save your entities.

When you return to the Processing Group maintenance form, click on the Get Staging Data menu item to start the import process.

When the Create Job dialog box is displayed, give your import process a description and then click on the OK button.

When the Staging Data Extraction dialog box is displayed, you can test your data by clicking on the Preview button within the menu bar.

After a second or two, you will be able to look at the View Staging Preview detail tab on the form and see all of the data has been staged for you.

To start the real import, click on the Run button within the menu bar. When the Staging dialog box is displayed, just click on the OK button.

You should get a notification of the number of records that have been staged.

To update the real tables within Dynamics AX, just click on the Copy Data To Target button within the menu bar.

When the Select a Job To Run dialog box is displayed, select the job that you just created, and then click on the OK button.

This will open up a Target Data Extraction dialog box. Just click on the Run button within the menu bar.

Then click on the OK button to start the import.

The Data Import Export Framework will do all of the hard work for you.

Now when you look at your table within Dynamics AX all of your new data will be ready for you to use.

How cool is that.

Restrict Field Access By Security Role

The roles within Dynamics AX are pre-configured to restrict users from accessing areas that they usually don't need to use, but you don't have to stop there. You can tweak the security even more by restricting access to the field level data that shows up on the forms through the security role maintenance feature, allowing you to give people read only access, or not even show the field in the case of sensitive information. As an added benefit, if you restrict access this way, then the users will not be able to access the data through the reports, or through the Excel add-in.

If your users are already paranoid that they don't see all of the data, then redacting access this way may push them over the edge.

How to do it...

Start off by finding the field that you want to restrict access to. In this case we want to stop particular users from maintaining the Vendors Bank Account.

Then find the Role that you want to restrict access through – in this example we are cheating a little and finding the Role through the user account, an then clicking on the Edit Role button within the User Roles tab.

When the Security Roles maintenance form is displayed, click on the Override Permissions button within the menu bar.

This will open up the Override Permissions form. To override the permissions on a table, click on the Table/Fields node.

This will allow you to browse all of the tables within Dynamics AX. Select the table that you want to restrict access to (in this case the VendTable) and expand it so that you can see all of the fields.

To override the permissions by field, select the parent table and then uncheck the Do Not Override checkbox.

This will allow you to override the general access to the table if you like. In this example though we will leave it with the Full control access level because we want to override the access to an individual field.

Now select the field that you want to restrict access to, and uncheck the Do Not Override checkbox.

Now you can change the access rights to that field by selecting the option from the Override Access Level dropdown box. You can set it to No Access, View, or Edit.

Now when the user returns to the form, they are not able to change the field if they belong to that security role.

Access Denied.

Copy Data Between Companies Quickly Using The Data Import Export Framework

The Data Import Export Framework module is not just for getting data in and out of Dynamics AX through import and export files, it also has a nifty feature that allows you to copy data within your companies, so if you are configuring a new legal entity for testing or production purposes, and want to populate it with information from another existing company, you can replicate the data in a matter of minutes.

It's like having your own personal Sketch-A-Graph, but not as much fun...

How to do it...

Just to set the stage for this example, we have one company that has a number of vendors loaded into one company.

And in another company the cupboards are bare...

To copy the data between the companies, click on the Copy Entity Data Between Companies menu item within the Common group of the Data Import Export Framework area page.

When the Copy Processing Group list page is displayed, click on the New button in the menu bar to create a new transfer.

This will start off a Copy Entity Wizard. Click the Next button to start the process.

When the Name The Copy Entity Processing Group page is displayed, give your record a Name and Description and then click on the Next button.

On the Select Entities To Copy page, select the Entities that you want to copy over from the Available Entities list box and then click on the > button to move them to the Entities To Copy side of the form.

In this case we are just selecting the Vendors, but if you wanted to populate an entirely new company with data from the existing one, then you could select everything if you liked.

When you have selected the Entities To Copy, click on the Next button to continue on.

On the Set Source And Destination Companies page, select the company that you want to copy from on the left hand side with the Available Source Companies, and also select the Target Companies on the right hand side where you wont to copy the data to.

Then click on the Next button.

If this is going to be a large update then you can specify the Batch details on the next page, but in this case we just click the Next button.

Now we have finished the configuration of the Copy Processing Group, we can click the Finish button to kick off the process.

After a short while, you will get a notification that the records have been copied within the two entities...

And if you look in the company that was missing the data, you will see all of the new data that you have created.

Now that's a heck of a lot easier than retyping in the data for sure.

Add Quick Links To Websites As Ribbon Bar Buttons

There are probably a lot of reference websites that you always go to during your day that you use in conjunction with Dynamics AX. Although it is not a big deal to open up your browser and type in the website address, you may want to make your life just a little bit easier and add the links to the pages directly within the Dynamics AX form that you are usually in when you need it. That way you are just a click away from the site rather than a couple of clicks and a lot of typing.

Although I wouldn't suggest that you add Farm Town as a link no matter how many crops you still have to harvest...

How to do it...

First, find the website that you want to open from the Dynamics AX ribbon bar.

Then find the form that you want to add a link to the website from.

Now we need to edit the form. A quick trick to find the form in AOT is to right-mouse-click on the form and select the Personalize option.

When the Personalization form is displayed, switch to the Information tab, and click on the Edit button to the right of the Form Name.

This will open up AOT and take you straight to the form that you need to modify.

Expand out the Design section and the ActionPane (a.k.a. the ribbon bar) and find the ribbon that you want to add the button to.

Right-mouse-click on the ActionPane, select the New Control submenu, and then select the ButtonGroup menu item.

This will add a new Button Group to the ribbon bar.

Hold down the ALT key and then use the Down Arrow key to move the button group to the bottom of the list.

Now we need to tidy up the button group. Start off by giving it a better Name value within the Properties panel.

Then right-mouse-click on the Button Group and select the New Control sub menu, and then select the Button menu item to create the button.

Now you will have a new Button control.

Change the Name for the button in the properties panel.

Then change the Text that will show for the button.

Change the ButtonDisplay property to Text & Image Below.

Then click on the ... button to the right of the NormalImage property and select an icon for the button.

Finally, we want a big image, so change the Big property to Yes.

Now expand the Button control, right-mouse-click on the Methods node, select the Override Method submenu, and then select the Clicked method so that we can tell it what to do when the button is clicked.

This will open up the method code editor.

Just add the following code to the beginning of the method:

Infolog.urllookup(http://yourwebsiteaddress);

After you have done that you can close the editor.

Now all that is left to do is to save the changes and close the form.

Now when you open up your form, there is an icon there for your website.

If you just click on it then Dynamics AX will open up your default browser and go straight to the site that your specified.

That is cool!

Deliver Blog Feeds Directly To Your Role Centers

Blogs are a great source of information, and come in many shapes and sizes ranging from external blogs that you may periodically access for inspiration and information, to internal blogs that you may have set up within your organization that give the employees updates on the happening within the company. For the more important blogs, you may want to add them to your Dynamics AX Role Center page so that they are delivered directly to you.

It's like your own personal newspaper delivery minus the neighbor that steals it before you get up.

How to do it...

First start off with the blog that you want to link to your role center.

Then find the RSS feed for the blog.

Tip: Usually you can find this by adding rss or feed to the end of the website URL.

Now open up Dynamics AX and open up your Role Center home page.

Then click on the Personalize This Page link in the top right of the form.

This will open the page up in personalization mode. You will notice some of the sections have a Add A Web Part link in them. Click on the one in the area that you want to add your blog post link.

When the web part browser is displayed, select the Content Rollup Category, select the RSS Viewer from the Web Parts list and then click on the Add button.

When you return to the Role Center page you will see that a new control has been added to the form, but it is not configured. Click on the Open The Tools Pane link.

This will open up the properties panel for the RSS Viewer web part on the right.

Within the RSS Properties group, paste in the URL for the RSS feed that you discovered earlier on.

Then within the Appearance group, change the Chrome State property to None. This will just remove the title from the web part which makes lit look tidier.

The default view of the blog post will look a little bland, so we will spiff it up a little by changing the format. To do this scroll right down to the bottom, and click on the XSL Editor button.

This will open up a Text Editor for the XSL.

Paste in the following code into the text editor.

Once you have done that, just click on the Save button to update the style sheet.

And then click on the OK button to save your changes

When the role center is updated you will notice that the blog post has been retrieved and is displayed in the designer mode.

All that you need to do now is click on the Stop Editing button within the Edit group of the Page ribbon bar.

Now you have an ultra-cool link directly to one of your favorite blog sites.

Make Users Feel Special By Creating New Role Centers For Their Unique Roles

Dynamics AX comes pre-packaged with over 40 standard role centers for a lot of the normal user types that you would expect to see within an organization – CFO, Salesperson, AP Clerk, etc. Chances are though you probably have roles within your organization that don't quite fit into those roles. You can either try to assign those users to one of the roles that most closely fits, or you can just create a new role centers especially for those users.

Say no to being generic.

How to do it...

Start off by browsing to one of your default Role Center pages.

Then from the Site Actions menu, click on the View All Site Content menu item.

When the Site Contents page is displayed, click on the Enterprise Portal document library.

When the Enterprise Portal library is displayed, you will be able to see all of the default Role Center templates. They are easy to spot and all begin with RoleCenter.

To create a new Role Center template click on the New Document menu item within the Documents tab on the ribbon bar.

This will open up the New Web Part Page creation page.

Give your Role Center Template a Name and then click on the Create button.

Note: You can change the layout of the template, but it is best just to use the default.

After the new Role Center Template is created, you will be taken into the edit mode for the page. To tweak the page, click on the Add a Web Part link on any of the columns .

This will open up the Web Part browser above the page. Select any of the standard web parts delivered with SharePoint and also Dynamics AX that you want to add to the page, and then click the Add button.

In this case we added the Cues control to the page.

You can continue adding Web Parts until you are satisfied with the template. Then click the Stop Editing button on the ribbon bar.

This will take you back to the view mode and you are done with the template creation.

The next step is to create a menu item for the Role Center within AOT. To do this you can go directly into the AOT tree and drill down into the URLs node within the Web Menu Items folder of the Web group.

Right-mouse-click on the URLs node and select the New URL menu item from the context menu.

This will create a new URL record for you that we will configure to point to the Role Center that you just created.

Give the URL object a Name, Label, and Help Text.

Within the URL property, type in the relative path for the Role Center that you created. It will probably be:

/Enterprise Portal/RoleCenterName.aspx

Also, make sure that you set the HomePage field to Yes. If you don't do this then the Role Center will open up in another window.

Once you have done that, then click the Save button in the tool bar to save the change.

Now we need to create a new User Profile. To do this, click on the User Profiles menu item within the Users folder of the Common group within the System Administration area page.

This will open up a list of all the User profiles in the system. Click on the New button within the menu bar to create a new record.

You can give your new profile a Name and a Description and from the drop down box on the Role Center field, you should be able to find the new Role Center menu that you just created.

Then click on the Users tab. To assign your users Profile click on the Add user button.

Now you can select the users that you want to assign to the role, and then click on the OK button.

Now you are done.

The next time your user logs in, their Role Center will be the new template that you created.

And your user is able to personalize their own custom custom role center.

Very cool.

Add Flair To Your Forms With Achievements

Achievements are everywhere you look. You can get them for checking into your favorite restaurant through Foursquare, you can get them for writing code within Visual Studio, and you can definitely get them on any game that you play on your phone. So why not add them to your Dynamics AX forms so that you can add a little pizazz to day.

In the immortal words of Stan... I need to talk about your flair.

How to do it...

Start off by finding the form that you want to add your achievements to.

Then right-mouse-click on the form, and select the Personalize option from the pop-up menu.

When the Personalization form is displayed, switch to the Information tab, and click on the Edit button to the right of the Form Name field.

This will open up AOT and with just the form that we selected showing in the explorer.

Expand out the Design section to the spot that you want to add your flair. In this case we will add it below the title on the form details.

Then right-mouse-click on the group form and select the New Control option from the pop-up-menu, and then choose the Button control.

This will add a new Button control to the group.

Within the Properties panel, update the Name.

Set the Button Display property to Image Only.

Then click on the ... to the right of the Image URL property so that you can browse and select an image to show for the button.

Set the Border to None so that the button shows up as a flat image... which looks nicer.

And finally, set the Back Style to Transparent so that it doesn't look like a button ☺

Now we need to create a method that we will use to tell Dynamics AX if we want to show the achievement button or not. To do this right-mouse-click on the Methods folder within the AOT and select the New Method menu item.

This will open up a new X++ editor window.

Replace the code within the method with the following code.

Once you have updated the code, you can close the editor.

Now we have all of the framework for our achievement. We just need to update the form to tell it to refresh for each record. To do this, expand out the Methods folder and double click on the UpdateControls method.

This will open up the X++ editor with the code that is ran every time the record is refreshed or changed.

Add the following code to the bottom of the method:

This.updateAchievements();

Once you have done that, save the updates and then close out of AOT.

Now when we open up the form, if the condition is met (in our case more than one order being placed for the customer) then everything looks normal.

But if they have met the criteria then it shows up.

How cool is that.

Choose Where To Go When You Click On Pop-Up Notifications

Pop-up notifications are great because it's like Dynamics AX is sending you a personalized gift every time they show up. You could be getting a personalized alert that you have set up, or being invited to help with workflow task to streamline the business. You can tweak what happens when you click on the link though to fit your personality. If you are more of an cautious person, then you have the link take you to the alert details where you can contemplate what you want to do. If you are more of a impulsive person, then you can throw all caution to the wind and just go straight to the transaction from the link and get things done right away.

Either way I am sure you will still be excited to see what the notification is...

How to do it...

To select what happens when you click on a notification from Dynamics AX, click on the Files menu, then select the Tools sub-menu, and then select the Options menu item.

When the Options dialog box is displayed, switch to the Notifications page and you will see a Pop-Up Link Destination field within the Alert Based Notifications field group. To go to the alert detail from the pop-ups, select the To Alert option and then click the Close button to exit from the form.

Now, wait for an alert to come through, and then click on it.

Clicking on the pop-up alert will take you to the alert details with the message information, and from here you can click on the Go To Origin button in the menu bar to navigate to the original transaction.

If you want to skip the alert screen and go straight to the transaction, the return to the Options page and change the Pop-Up Link Destination to To Alert Origin.

Now wait for an alert to come through and click it.

Now you will go straight to the transaction that initiated the alert.

Ripping wrapping paper off presents is much more fun.

Declutter Your System By Turning Off License Features You Don't Use

Dynamics AX is chock full of useful features, but you probably don't need to use it all right away, and in some cases even through other people will need a particular feature you may never consider using it. Rather than having everything enabled within the system, you can use the license configuration tool to deactivate is so that it's not showing up on the forms, and the menus. Later on if you find that you want to use the feature then you can always just turn it back on again.

Don't be an extreme hoarder when it comes to ERP features.

How to do it...

To do this, click on the License Configuration menu item within the Licensing folder of the Setup group within the System Administration area page.

When the License Configuration maintenance form is displayed, you will be able to see all of the different configuration options that are available within the system.

Tip: Before you continue on, just click on the Export To button and save your current configuration just in case you want to restore all of the features back to the same state that you currently have them in.

Now you can go through all of the different options, and turn off the features that you don't need. If you want to be super simple, then just click on the Standard button to turn off all but the bare necessities.

After you have tidied up the license options, click on the OK button, and you will be asked to synchronize the database with the license files. This will go through all of the tables, and make any necessary adjustments for you.

You may want to get a coffee while this is running.

After the synchronization has completed, you will notice that there are not as many bells and whistles configured in the system. For example, by turning off the Catch Weight options, the sales order screen looks a lot more compact.

With all of the options turned on, there is a lot more columns available for you to hide.

Just as a side note, if you can't kick the habit of turning on all of the features, then you can also feed your compulsive disorder by looking through the licensing file to see what options you are missing.

To make sure that you're not missing out, you can enable some more features.

And like magic, you now have new features that you may not have known that you can take advantage of.

Add Menu Items To The Tools Menu

You probably know already that you can create your own menu items and menus within Dynamics AX, but in addition to being able to update the navigation menus for the area pages, you can also update the Tools menu as well to add any utilities and forms that you may want users to access. This way the users don't have to have access to AOT in order to open up those common hidden utilities.

If you really want to be clever, you can even add Tetris.

How to do it...

Start off by opening up AOT and finding the menu item that you want to add to the Tool menu.

Now we will want to create a menu item for the form. To do this navigate to the Menu Items folder within AOT, right-mouse-click on the Display node, and then select the New Menu Item menu item.

This will create a new menu item element for you.

Give the new menu item a Name and a Label and then from the Object dropdown list, select the form that you want to add to the menu.

You don't have to make any more changes to the Menu Item control.

Now we want to add the menu item to the Tools menu. To do this, expand the Menus folder within AOT and find the GlobalToolsMenu item within the menus.

Right-mouse-click on the GlobalToolsMenu item, select the New menu item and then click on the Menu Item menu item.

This will create a new menu item node within the GlobalToolsMenu.

From the MenuItemName dropdown box in the Properties panel, find the new menu item that you just created.

This will automatically populate the Name property for you from the Menu Item details.

All you need to do now is click on the Save button to update the code.

Now when you open up the Tools submenu menu you will see your new menu item there.

Clicking on it will open up the menu item.

That's too simple.

Create Composite Menus That Combine Functions From Multiple Areas

As you use Dynamics AX more and more, you will find that you are sometimes using some functions from one area of the system, and then other features from another area in order to complete a task. Although everything is in the logical place, you may want to have a way to access everything at once from one menu. That's not a problem though, you can easily create your own menu groups that meld multiple areas into one single location to make it easier to find everything that you want.

And you don't even have to wait for lightening in order to make it come alive.

How to do it...

In this example we want to create a menu that is joins two areas into a single menu. The first is the Service Management menu.

And the second is the Project Management and Accounting menu.

To start off, open up AOT and expand the Menus node in the tree.

Right-mouse-click on the Menus node and select the New Menu menu item.

This will create a new Menu for you.

In the Properties panel, assign the menu a Name and also a Label.

To make this menu look like the other ones we will assign it an icon. To do this, change the ImageLocation field to EmbeddedResource so that we can use the existing icons within the system.

Then select the NormalImage field and click on the ... icon to the right of the field.

This will open up the Embedded Resources browser and you can scroll through to find the icon that you want to use and then just copy the resource id into the NormalImage property field.

Also, change the SetCompany field to Yes.

Now we want to add our new menu to the main menu. To do this scroll down within the Menu group and expand the MainMenu menu.

Right-mouse-click on the MainMenu node and select the New and then the Menu Reference menu item.

This will open up a Select Menus panel.

All you need to do is drag the new menu that you just created over to the MainMenu.

The menu will be added to the bottom of the menu. To rearrange it, just select the menu reference and then use the ALT+UPARROW to move the menu up in the list.

Then close down the Select Menu pane.

Next we want to add the sub-menus to our menu. To do this, right=mouse-click on the new menu that you created and select the Open New Window menu item.

This will create a new window with just that menu it it and you can then tile the windows so that you see the original AOT explorer, and then the menu that you are creating.

Expand out the menu that you want to copy the menu items from, and then while holding down the CTRL key (so that you copy and not move) drag the sub-menu that you want within the new menu over into the mew menu's window.

In this case I don't want all of the sub-folders within that group, so just delete all of the ones that are not necessary. This is easier than copying the menu items one by one.

After you have deleted all of the items that you don't need then your menu should look a little simpler.

Repeat the process for all of the other sub-folders of the menu.

Now expand out the second menu that you want to combine together with the first one and repeat the process.

After a few minutes you should have a new composite menu. After rearranging the main menu groups, just save the menu by pressing CTRL+S.

The next time that you log into Dynamics AX you will now see your new menu.

And when you open up the menu you will see all of the menu items that you want and just the menu items that you want.

Now I have a Contracts Management menu item.

SUMMARY

There are so many tricks and tips that you can take advantage of within Dynamics AX, that we cannot possibly inventory them all, but the ones that we have shown throughout this book are a good start.

About The Author

Murray Fife is an author of over 25 books on Microsoft Dynamics AX including the Bare Bones Configuration Guide Series which contains over 15 books that show novice users host to set up Dynamics AX using visual walkthroughs. These guides start off with the Financial modules of Dynamics AX and then progress through the Operational, Distribution, and then the more specialized modules like production, service management, and project accounting. You can find all of his books on Amazon here www.amazon.com/author/murrayfife.

Additionally, he is the curator of the Dynamics AX Companions (www.dynamicsaxcompanions.com) site which he built from the ground up as a resource for all of the Dynamics AX community where you can find walkthroughs and blueprints that he created since first being introduced to the Dynamics AX product.

Throughout his 25+ years of experience in the software industry he has worked in many different roles during his career, including as a developer, an implementation consultant, a trainer and a demo guy within the partner channel which gives him a great understanding of the requirements for both customers and partners perspective.

For more information on Murray, here is his contact information:

Email:	mcf@dynamicsaxcompanions.com
Twitter:	@murrayfife
Facebook:	facebook.com/murraycfife
Google:	google.com/+murrayfife
LinkedIn:	linkedin.com/in/murrayfife
Blog:	atinkerersnotebook.com
Docs:	docs.com/mufife
Amazon:	amazon.com/author/murrayfife

Need More Help with Dynamics AX

We are firm believers that Dynamics AX is not a hard product to learn, but the problem is where do you start. Which is why we developed the Bare Bones Configuration Guides. The aim of this series is to step you though the configuration of Dynamics AX from a blank system, and then step you through the setup of all of the core modules within Dynamics AX. We start with the setup of a base system, then move on to the financial, distribution, and operations modules. Each book builds upon the previous ones, and by the time you have worked through all of the guides then you will have completely configured a simple (but functional) Dynamics AX instance. To make it even more worthwhile you will have a far better understanding of Dynamics AX and also how everything fits together.

As of now there are 16 guides in this series broken out as follows:
- Configuring a Base Dynamics AX Test System
- Configuring an Organization within Dynamics AX
- Configuring the General Ledger within Dynamics AX
- Configuring Cash and Bank Management within Dynamics AX
- Configuring Accounts Receivable within Dynamics AX
- Configuring Accounts Payable within Dynamics AX
- Configuring Product Information Management within Dynamics AX
- Configuring Inventory Management within Dynamics AX
- Configuring Procurement and Sourcing within Dynamics AX
- Configuring Sales Order Management within Dynamics AX
- Configuring Human Resource Management within Dynamics AX
- Configuring Project Management and Accounting within Dynamics AX
- Configuring Production Control within Dynamics AX

- Configuring Sales and Marketing within Dynamics AX
- Configuring Service Management within Dynamics AX
- Configuring Warehouse Management within Dynamics AX

Although you can get each of these guides individually, and we think that each one is a great Visual resources to step you through each of the particular modules, for those of you that want to take full advantage of the series, you will want to start from the beginning and work through them one by one. After you have done that you would have done people told me was impossible for one persons to do, and that is to configure all of the core modules within Dynamics AX.

If you are interested in finding out more about the series and also view all of the details including topics covered within the module, then browse to the Bare Bones Configuration Guide landing page on the Dynamics AX Companions (www.dynamicsaxcompanions.com) website. You will find all of the details, and also downloadable resources that help you with the setup of Dynamics AX. Here is the full link:

http://www.dynamicsaxcompanions.com

www.ingramcontent.com/pod-product-compliance
Lightning Source LLC
Chambersburg PA
CBHW071406050326
40689CB00010B/1770

* 9 7 8 1 5 3 9 3 1 6 0 0 8 *